D0422231

DISCARD

4 .07

The Bookbinder

The Bookbinder

More Stories from the Road

Jackie K. Cooper

Mercer University Press

Macon, Georgia

Columbus Public Library

ISBN 978-0-88146-023-0
MUP/H702

© 2006 Mercer University Press
1400 Coleman Avenue
Macon, Georgia 31207
All rights reserved

First Edition.

The paper used in this publication meets the minimum requirements of
American National Standard for Information Sciences—Permanence of
Paper for Printed Library Materials, ANSI Z39.48-1992.

Library of Congress Cataloging-in-Publication Data

Cooper, Jackie K.
The book binder : more stories from the road / Jackie K. Cooper. --
1st
ed.
p. cm.
ISBN-13: 978-0-88146-023-0 (hardback : alk. paper)
ISBN-10: 0-88146-023-0 (hardback : alk. paper)
1. Cooper, Jackie K. 2. Perry (Ga.)—Biography—Anecdotes.
3. Critics—Georgia—Perry—Anecdotes.
4. Journalists—Georgia—Perry—Anecdotes. I. Title.
CT275.C775142A3 2004b
975.8'515092—dc22
[B]
2006017038

Columbus Public Library

For my sons J. J. and Sean and their wives Angela and Paula.

They got the best of me.

Contents

Acknowledgments

My stories are generally based on the important memories of my life. My thanks to all those who have helped me relive the past and added their memories to mine. This includes my immediate family, my closest friends, and even the strangers who called to add comments and stories to my collection.

I also want to thank Marc Jolley and his staff at Mercer University Press, my typist Louann Lucas, my encouragers who are also known as the "lunch bunch," and all my fellow writers who have helped so much just by sharing their writing experiences with me.

And as always I have to thank my mother who told me I was special, and my wife who makes me feel that I am.

Introduction

By Jaclyn Weldon White

A visit from an old friend is one of life's greatest joys. And Jackie K. Cooper is just the kind of person you'd like to find on your doorstep. Every time you pick up *The Bookbinder*, you're inviting this master storyteller into your home. So pull a comfortable chair up to the fire and let Jackie tell you some stories.

He has a knack for finding the common threads among us. When he shares memories of playing with friends in the long-ago summer twilights of South Carolina, you'll almost believe the story is about your own childhood. Surely that was you and *your* friends playing dodge ball or scaring yourselves silly with ghost stories. These tales strike such old familiar chords that you'll nearly be able to taste the snow cones or hear your mother's voice calling you home over the years.

In many ways, Jackie Cooper is just us. You may find yourself laughing out loud as he hides his cash in his shoe to avoid muggers at the airport or becomes the victim of a vicious vending machine that threatens to rip his clothes from his body. You'll most likely identify with Cooper as he takes on the everyday worries of the world. How often have any of us lamented the prevalence of surly sales clerks or complained about the sorry state of today's manners? Who hasn't stayed up hours past bedtime waiting to hear that a loved one has safely reached a distant destination or worried about the health of aging parents? Sure, we've all been there. But Jackie serves up these ordinary concerns in insightful slices of life that leave his readers chuckling or even brushing away a tear.

Of course, not every story in *The Bookbinder* will be familiar. One of the things that is so intriguing about reconnecting with old friends is discovering just how divergent your paths have become. And there is one particular area where Jackie Cooper is different from you and me. His work as a movie and book critic has carried him to glamorous places and allowed him to mingle with celebrities on a regular basis.

Go with him to Hollywood and New York. Sit back as he encounters the likes of James Earl Jones, Shirley MacLaine, and William Diehl. He'll take you behind the scenes of the press junkets and movie premieres that the rest of us only see from a distance.

In addition to meeting the real stars of the day, Cooper seems to be a magnet for the wannabe celebrities that crowd into the show business capitals. Let him introduce you to the Los Angeles cab driver who holds his riders hostage with lengthy descriptions of the screenplays he has written and hopes to sell just as soon as he gets that big break. And squirm right along with Jackie when, while waiting for a delayed flight out of La Guardia, he runs into a stage mother who insists on having her six-year-old daughter belt out a rousing rendition of "Tomorrow" from *Annie*, right there at the check-in counter.

There is no doubt you're going to enjoy *The Bookbinder*. When you finish, it will seem as if an old friend has taken his leave. But you'll never forget Jackie Cooper or his stories. Oprah Winfrey once described him as "a gentle man." She was right, but she didn't go far enough. He is a gentle, caring man who is completely in love with his family, his friends, and his life. Once you've read his book, you'll be glad to count this gentle man among your own "old friends."

Prologue

When I was a child someone told me that everything I did was making a memory. I didn't have a clue as to what they were talking about. I just sort of smiled and then went outside to play. Until recently I hadn't even thought of "making memories." That is not until I went to speak to a high school English class and was taking questions from the students. One of them asked me if my books were autobiographical. I answered that they were somewhat that way but they were mostly memoirs.

"Memoirs!" A light clicked on and I realized my books are mostly memories, memories I have been making all my life. I didn't start out to write my life story from birth till now, I created books primarily based on those happenings that had been imprinted on my mind. So that is what you are holding here—my memories. They are taken from the journals I have kept all my life, and the one you have in your hand are particularly focused on 1996, 1997, and 1998. The years 1996 and 1998 bookend a seminal event in my life: my youngest son's wedding in 1997. I am sure many of you can relate to how an event like that can be the happiest and the saddest time of your life. Relating is the source of what this book is intended to do. It is aimed at making you reflect back or ponder over an event in your own life that we share in common. Maybe that reflection will make you smile or it might even bring a tear.

Whatever the reaction, I hope it is a bond between you the reader and me the writer.

A few years ago I was selling books at the Cherry Blossom Festival in Macon, Georgia. A lady came into the booth and told me she had read all my books. She then asked me if I knew what she called them. I couldn't imagine what word she would use, but several negative choices raced through my mind. Still I managed to ask her what she did call them, and she answered "my comfort books." It seems she read a story whenever she had had a bad day, or when she just needed a pick me up. She then added, "You write stories that bind us together."

I was so flattered by that statement, and I thought about it long and hard when I got home. I realized I had reached my goal, as I had always wanted my stories to be a means to bind people together or to make them relate to events I described. I also decided at that moment that my next book would be titled *The Bookbinder*. Hopefully it too would be a gathering of stories that would bind people together through shared memories.

Our journey through life is not always easy, and sometimes the load can only be lightened by sharing our experiences with others we meet along the way. Knowing we are not alone in this adventure makes it easier to understand. So enter the world of *The Bookbinder* knowing it is one man's recollection of the memories he has made so far on this planet. Read them, enjoy them, and let the past wash over you as we seek a means to bind ourselves to each other and the whole community of mankind.

Chapter 1

Reflections from Route 96

The Best of Times and the Worst of Times

My Christmas experience this year was something Dickens might have been referring to when he spoke of the best of times and the worst of times. It didn't start out that way. On the surface everything appeared to be headed for a normal family Christmas...but then things changed.

The plans had been for my folks to come to our home in Perry on Christmas Eve and go back to South Carolina the day after Christmas. But on Saturday morning, December 23, my stepmother called and said her brother had died the night before.

I had known my stepmother's brother Grady all my life. He and his wife had lived up the street from us, and his four daughters had been like sisters to my brother and myself. Grady was eighty-three years old and had been in failing health for more than a decade, but it was still rough on my stepmother to let him go, especially at Christmas time.

The funeral was set for 2:00 P.M. on Christmas Eve so Terry and I drove up to South Carolina that morning. When we got there the expression on my stepmother's face made the entire trip worthwhile. Although she had told us not to come, she obviously was thrilled that we had, and she thanked us over and over again.

Grady's oldest daughter still lives in Clinton, and the other three sisters live in various cities in South Carolina so they were all there. And they all had their families with them. It was a huge crowd and a gregarious one. I met new people right and left, trying to keep straight who belonged to who.

The Adair girls are named Linda, Judy, Sue, and Trudy. I always enjoyed introducing them and hearing the rhyme it produced. Judy and I are just about the same age. We have been friends forever and she calls me "her first love." Her husband William is a good sport about hearing that, but I always look around to see where he is when she makes this declaration. If he's not in sight, then I always respond with "I love you too, Judy."

Since it was Christmas, a lot of people from the old neighborhood were home. It was the first time I had seen some of them since high school. One of the "girls" from up the street was at the funeral and I was amazed at how good she still looked. She is older than I am, which puts her between forty and death.

I went up to her after the graveside service and put my arm around her. She looked at me like I was some sort of crazy man. "Mary Ann," I said, "don't you remember me?"

She looked at me closely and was as blank as a wall. I saw her confusion so I quickly said, "It's me, Jackie Cooper."

She gave me a loud laugh and cried, "I don't believe it! Is it really? You have gotten so old!"

Thanks a lot, Mary Ann, I thought. *You are older than I am, honey!* But I didn't say anything, just hugged her and told her how glad I was to see her.

Then she said it again. "You are an old man!"

My smile was beginning to fade. And then the fool said it again. At this point my wife had heard enough. "I think you have said that enough," she said between clenched teeth.

The point was made. Mary Ann finally moved on to another subject and we had a nice chat. Terry never was too friendly to Mary Ann.

During that visit to Clinton, I saw more people from my childhood than I had seen in ages. So even though I hated the loss of Grady, I still enjoyed the visit. It was the best of times. It was the worst of times.

Play the Sunset

Call us cynics, but it has become a running joke with my family that when we hear the TV announcer state in ominous tones a certain show will be "very special" we all get smirky looks on our faces. We have heard that so many times as in "a very special *Highway to Heaven*" or "a very special *Different Strokes*." Saying something is going to be "very special" doesn't always mean it is going to be of extra entertainment value.

So with this in mind I am very hesitant to say a movie is "very special" but I am going out on a limb and saying it anyway. *Mr. Holland's Opus* is a very special movie. In this day and age of extreme sensationalism, a movie like this one is a rarity indeed.

Mr. Holland's Opus stars Richard Dreyfus as a musician who takes a teaching job at a high school so he can support himself and his wife while he is composing.

Of course, as with most career choices, things do not go as planned. Holland (Dreyfus) and his wife start their family and have bills that always need to be paid. And, surprisingly, as Mr. Holland gets more and more involved with his students and their music, he finds he does not want to rush away for another career.

The point of *Mr. Holland's Opus* is that the life of teaching he gives to his students is his symphony. Now that may sound a little corny and overdone, but it is true in this movie and it is true in real life: teachers do create a whole score of musical lives with their influence.

Maybe it's because my wife is a teacher and my brother was a teacher that I have these feelings. I know how much effort they expend to try to give a positive influence and a broadening of knowledge to the students who come within their sphere. And it has always been so.

My teachers in school were some of the most positive role models I have ever had. I remember Miss Shealy who taught me to love to read. She brought the English language to life for me. Then there was Mr. Bouknight who tried to make me love to play the clarinet. He never did succeed, but he did give me a better appreciation of music. And there was also Miss Wallace who showed me how Latin is the root of many, many of today's words. I have never forgotten my Latin roots.

Each of these teachers played a part in my life in high school and their memories still stay with me today. I am sure I am just one of many who reflect back on each of their teaching skills and personalities. A lot of years have passed since I was under their influence, but the lessons and ideas they gave me still linger in my mind.

One of the most impressive scenes in *Mr. Holland's Opus* occurs when Holland is trying to teach young Alicia Witt to enjoy playing the clarinet. He is trying to find something in her being that can be expressed in her playing. He asks her what she considers her best feature and she answers her red hair, because her father says it looks like the sunset. With great emotion, he tells her to "Play the sunset."

That is what teachers do for us. They teach us to "play the sunset" in all areas of our lives. They enrich us, they inspire us, they mold us. *Mr. Holland's Opus* captures the spirit of teachers and makes this movie a tribute to all of them who have so inspired us.

It is "a very special movie."

I Wish Her Well

Here it is Valentine's Day again and romance is in the air. Well, at least for some of us it is. I have considered myself to be a romantic all of my life, in the sense that I have a deep-seated need to love and be loved.

Thankfully I am now married with children and out of the dating game. Would I like to be back there? Not on your life! I remember the heartaches of young love all too well. And I wouldn't want to go back through it. One time was definitely enough.

In Clinton, South Carolina, where I was born and raised, we dated young. It seems we were pairing off from grammar school on. I can remember that when I first started dating my mother had to drive my date and me to the movie—and I started driving at fourteen! That was then and this is now, and I sure wouldn't let any child of mine start dating at that age.

My first serious girlfriend was Elaine. When we started dating I was fifteen and she was thirteen. The first date we had was to the movies and she had to be home by 9:30 P.M. It was go to the movies, race to get something to eat, then take her home.

We dated for five years, and we had plans to get married. Since she was two years behind me, we had it all worked out about college. When she graduated from high school I would be finishing my sophomore year at Erskine College. Then she would go to Winthrop College and take a two-year business course, which would put us both graduating at the same time. We would get married the summer after we graduated, and then I would go to law school and she would get a job as a secretary.

The problem with this grand plan was that Elaine did not care much for college. After a few months at Winthrop she called and said she didn't like school and thought it was a waste of time since we planned to get married. She thought since she had graduated from high school we should go on and tie the knot. I disagreed.

The next time I went up to see her she was very cool. It was our first big argument. Once again she said she thought we should get married. Once again I argued for waiting. I tried to convince her we would starve to death if we got married while I was still in college.

The next weekend it was all over. When I went up to see her, she took off the ring I had given her for Valentine's Day when she was in the ninth grade. It had never been off her finger, even though it turned it a serious shade of green.

The ring coming off was a true sign our romance was dead. And it was. She dropped out of college and was engaged to someone else by Christmas. I couldn't believe it. I continued to call her, but she wouldn't change her mind. She had found someone who loved her enough to marry her.

The funny thing is she didn't get married until the June after I graduated. That was supposed to be our wedding month. Everyone in Clinton said they couldn't believe it wasn't us getting married. It had been Jackie and Elaine for so long.

Did it take me a long time to get over this hurt? Did it ever. I didn't meet Terry until seven years later. But once I found her I knew the Jackie/Elaine scenario was never meant to be. Still, the years before I found my true love were miserable.

So would I like to be dating again? Never. I'll take the joy of my life now and never look back. As for Elaine, she and her husband have two children and three grandchildren and have lived happily ever after.

God bless her, I wish her well.

Sweet Memories

When I was thinking back about Elaine and our high school romance, it started me thinking about the Erskine girls I dated. Erskine College is located in Due West, South Carolina, and is known throughout the state for having some of the prettiest co-eds around. And during my four years at Erskine they had a bumper crop. Does that sound sexist? Well, I don't mean it in any derogatory sense. I mean it as purely complimentary.

One of the first girls I dated at Erskine was named Lynn. She was a sophomore when I was a freshman so she was "an older woman." Lynn was one of those people who is fresh-faced and appealing in a Doris Day sense. She exuded wholesomeness. I was crazy about her from the moment I met her.

What later cemented our friendship was the commonality of our pasts. Lynn had lost her mother at an early age and had a stepmother with whom she did not get along. We shared our anger and our grief.

I was also always amazed at Lynn's gumption. Whenever there was a talent presentation for a chapel program Lynn was there. She had a nice voice, but when she performed she mimed a song that had been recorded by some talented person. There she would be, up on the stage, looking like she was singing her heart out, but in reality she was just moving her mouth and letting some professional do all the work. It might sound a little corny or cheesy but with Lynn it worked. She provided the personality while someone else provided the voice.

Lynn and I dated on and off until she graduated then we lost touch with each other. Years later I moved to Georgia and discovered Lynn lived a few miles from me in Macon. Now we see or talk to each other pretty regularly. She is married and has three sons. I don't think she lip syncs any more but I really haven't asked her.

Ann was another girl I dated at Erskine. I met her my sophomore year when she was a freshman. Ann told me from the start she had a boyfriend back in Fort Mill, South Carolina, and they were serious. Elaine and I had just broken up so I was ready for a new love. I dreamed that Ann would fall for me, but she stayed true to the Fort Mill guy.

The thing that impressed me most about Ann was that when we danced together she placed her hand on the back of my neck. Now don't ask me why that made such an impression on me, but it did. I have never been that much of a dancer, but with her I could have danced and danced and danced.

Lynda was the last serious relationship I had at Erskine. She was one of the most stunning people I have ever met, just drop-dead gorgeous. Plus she had a sense of humor that nobody expected and that she didn't show to everyone. But as I got to know her, I found her humor hysterical. Beauty and a sense of humor—to me that was a deadly combination.

Lynda and I dated on and off for a year and then she transferred to Georgia Southern in Statesboro, Georgia. I have often wondered what happened to her. But that was years ago and our paths have never crossed.

Each relationship we have prepares us for the next one. I was slowly making my way to the time when I would meet Terry, who would become my wife. We live, we learn, we become. Hindsight helps us see why each relationship would not have been the one for a lifetime. Still the memories are sweet and I wouldn't trade them for anything.

The One Vote Loss

Recently I was talking with one of my fiends in another town. He was telling me that his daughter had been in a high school beauty pageant and had not won. He said she was crushed because she really thought she should win. He said she had done all the things she thought were necessary to make a good showing—the new dress, the hairdo, etc. But to no avail.

This got me to thinking about when I was in high school and how my friends and I plotted to win senior superlatives. Back in those days the senior class voted among itself to name the "best" of this and that. It was considered a big honor since only about 10 of our class of 100 would be selected.

My group decided we would block vote for the superlatives in order to guarantee as much success as possible. Each one of us picked the category in which we thought we stood the best chance. Margaret wanted to be "Most Popular" which was a shoo-in because everybody knew she was. Hollis opted for "Best Personality," and Chuck went for "Wittiest." We insisted that Charlotte pick "Best-Looking" because, again, we knew she was.

As for me, I knew I wasn't "Best Looking" material. And I thought wanting "Best Personality" seemed a little vain. So I decided my best chance was in the category of "Most Likely to Succeed."

We all campaigned for each other so that none of us would have to campaign for himself/herself. We spread the word and then sat back to wait for the results.

The first day of balloting was for "Most Popular." We voted and then waited for the votes to be counted. The next day there was an announcement that Margaret was the most popular girl, and there was a runoff between Peyton Howser and me for most popular boy. I was stunned. Peyton Howser was our senior class president!

We voted again that morning and I had my fingers crossed hoping against hope that I would win. That afternoon, my English teacher, Miss Shealy called me into her room and told me I had lost—by one vote!

As I was leaving school that day, a friend of mine came up to me and said she had wanted to vote for me for "Most Popular," but she had been told I really wanted "Most Likely To Succeed." She didn't vote for me. Her one vote would have been one less for Peyton and one more for me. I would have won.

By being so conniving as to plot to win my superlative I had ruined my chance of being voted "Most Popular." Sometimes it is just better to let nature take its course.

As I am writing this, something has just occurred to me. Miss Shealy was the type of teacher who never wanted to hurt anyone's feelings. When she asked you a question and you gave the wrong answer, she would say sweetly, "No, but thank you for trying." I bet I missed out on that "Most Popular" selection by a much wider margin than one vote. Miss Shealy, being as kind as she was, probably wanted me to have the comfort of it being so close so she fibbed that I was only one vote shy of a win.

What a great gift. I have lived on that one vote loss for years.

My Middle-Aged Friend

I want to tell you about my friend Marvin. Marvin is my middle-aged friend. That does not mean that he is middle-aged but that we became friends in my middle age. If you are not aware of it yet (due to your age), you will soon learn that the friends of your youth and the friends of your middle age are different.

When I was young my friends were people I saw daily, for hours each day. When I was growing up Chuck, Hollis, and I were inseparable. We went to grammar school, high school, and college together. But the friends of my middle age are different.

I still feel as strongly about them, but I see them maybe once a week; or even once every other week. With the hustle and bustle of everyday life and work, that is all the time I have to spare.

I met Marvin through his wife, Linda, with whom I judged the Miss Senior Warner Robins contest a few years ago. She is a charming lady full of life and vitality. In our conversation it came up that I had a movie club. Linda said that sounded like fun and asked me to send her information about it. I did and she became a member.

During the first session she attended, she brought her husband as a guest one night. Marvin loved movies, too, and when the next class started he became a member. And a welcome one he was.

People enjoyed Marvin being in the club because: (1) he always had an opinion about the movies he had seen, and (2) he always had a funny story to tell about something that had happened to him when he saw it. He was warm, witty, and just all-around charming. I enjoyed him to the fullest.

A few weeks ago as the Macon movie club was winding down Marvin missed a meeting. I asked Linda about him, and she said he was going in for some surgery.

The next week the group went out to a movie and to eat afterward, and Marvin and Linda didn't attend. Marvin was in the hospital by that time recovering from cancer surgery.

I called Marvin the next day in the hospital and fussed at him for not coming to our movie club social. He laughed and said he had had another appointment that precluded it. But he told me not to take him off my movie club roster. He was going to have some chemotherapy, but he would still attend most of the club meetings. I told him he had better.

Sadly, in less than two weeks I had a call from another movie club member saying Marvin had died. I was stunned. I just couldn't believe death could have come so quickly.

It was with a heavy heart that I went to Marvin's funeral. As the service at the funeral home chapel started, music filled the air. It was the theme from *Somewhere in Time*. Later more music was played, this time Barbara Streisand singing *The Way We Were*. These songs were so appropriate because they spoke of the great love between Marvin and Linda and they were from movies that he loved so much.

The loss of friends from your middle age are just as heart wrenching as the loss of friends from your youth.

Marvin came into my life late but I will certainly miss him. As a Christian, I know that "somewhere in time" I will see him just "the way he was."

I Want to Be a Star

A few weeks ago I was in California to interview Richard Gere for an upcoming movie. When I landed in Los Angeles, the studio sent a driver and car out to take me to my hotel (It's a tough job, but somebody has to do it.).

I have never been comfortable with this limousine and driver thing. The first time I had a car meet me, I hopped in the front seat with the driver. He very courteously told me he thought I would be more comfortable in the back seat. Now, I always sit in the back seat but lean over the front seat to carry on a conversation.

All of the drivers are actors or writers waiting for their big break in the movies. This one was no exception. He was an actor with the name of "Boss" Johnson. He hadn't gotten his big break yet, but it should be happening any day. I hope so since this guy looked older than I did.

He had been an attorney in Virginia with a wife and two children when he decided to chuck it all and head for the lights of LA. I got the impression the wife and two kids did not make the move with him.

He said he had made some good connections in Los Angeles and was waiting for a call back on the new Johnny Depp movie "Donnie Brasco." He said he had a role as an FBI agent nailed down. The call should come any moment.

The driver on the ride back to the airport was a writer. He had a script that was being looked at by Robert Duvall and George C. Scott. Or, as he put it, his people had sent it to their people.

He said his script was unique and that it would make a fascinating movie if Hollywood only had the guts to film it. He didn't want to tell me too much about the plot because then someone may copy it and get theirs filmed first. I guess I looked like I was going to run out and sell the story to the first person I met on the street. When I asked him about the plot, he said politely, "No offense, but I had better just keep that to myself."

My last Hollywood-hopeful story took place at the Four Seasons Hotel. The night of my arrival, the studio had a cocktail party there. The waitress serving my table was a very pretty young blonde. I was telling the other writers there about my driver and his "want to be an actor" story. I ended by saying that I thought everyone working in Hollywood was an actor in search of a job.

I turned to the waitress when she came to the table and said, "I bet you are an actress." I really was joking but she quickly answered, "Yes, I am. My name is Jennifer Aspen (as in the city) and I play Greg Brady's girlfriend in the next 'Brady Bunch' movie."

She also rattled off a list of soap operas and sitcoms she had done. As she cleared away our plates she smiled and said, "Remember that is Jennifer Aspen, A-S-P-E-N."

Mark that name down. She is bound to be a big star some day. At least I hope so. Everyone who follows his or her dream deserves some measure of success—even Hollywood wannabes.

The Engagement

Terry and I have been gaga over our boys since the days they were born. In every respect they have been everything we wanted them to be and more, much more. Having two sons, we've been lucky to have one who looks like her side of the family and one who looks like mine.

Although our oldest is the "junior," it is the youngest who looks like me. Sean, the baby boy, and I are more alike in looks and temperament, while J. J., the eldest son, has the Millard olive skin and complexion. These boys are as different-looking as day and night, but they are both fine.

It's funny that we ended up with two boys since I really wanted to have a daughter. I have no sisters, so I thought a little girl would be just wonderful for our family. Of course, when J. J. was born I was so thrilled that he was normal and perfect that I never had a moment's disappointment that he wasn't a girl.

But when we found out we were going to have another child, I really did hope for a girl. What we got was another baby boy who was, and still is, the sweetest dispositioned person you will ever want to know. He also grew and grew and grew. Yes, Sean started out small but almost overnight got to be a big one. He was so big that it seemed incongruous for his mother to call him "Precious" or for me to call him "Pooh."

I remember when he was playing football for Westfield High School. People in the stands would pick up the cheers for "Precious." I'm sure Sean could have died from mortification, but he never let on that it bothered him.

Last Monday I was driving to Biloxi with a friend when my car phone rang. It was Terry telling me that she and Sean had been shopping and had found a ring for him to give his girlfriend. Sean had turned twenty-one a few days earlier and had decided it was time to get engaged. The wedding won't be for a year, but he wanted to give the ring now.

When I got back from Biloxi, I saw the ring, and it is pretty. He hadn't given it to his girlfriend Paula yet and thought he might wait until Easter. But then the time seemed right and he went ahead and presented her with it.

This means that in a year I will finally have a girl in my family, and she is pretty special too. I think from the moment they met they knew they were right for each other. Or as someone told me, God took Sean's rib and made Paula to be his perfect match.

It's hard for me to accept that my boys are old enough to even think about marriage, but it happens. Time flies and the heart expands. There is room there for one more—the daughter my baby boy is bringing me.

Movie Mania

It simply amazes me when I find people who love going to the movies as much or more than I do. Since I started my movie clubs in Macon, Warner Robins, and Dublin, I have been exposed to people who are real movie fans. They can talk movies from the most superficial aspects to the most detailed and always bring up points that I missed.

Last week my Dublin group came to Macon to see a movie and to go out to eat together. There were twelve of them and they went to see *Primal Fear* with Richard Gere. I had already seen the movie in California so I spent the time setting up arrangements with the restaurant for us to eat later.

When I got back to the theater to wait for my group to get out, I saw two ladies walking around the lobby. I struck up a conversation with them, as I am known to do, and found out they were waiting for *Mr. Holland's Opus* to start. One of the ladies had already seen it, but she wanted to see it with her friend.

The more I talked with them the more amazed I was. Not only were they going to see *Mr. Holland's Opus*, but they had already seen *A Family Thing*, *Faithful* and *Diabolique*. Okay, so had I. But these two ladies had seen them all that day! They had started at noon and were working their way through the day. I couldn't help but ask if they had survived on popcorn the whole day.

It seems the two ladies had been friends when they both lived in Warner Robins. One of the ladies still did, but the other had moved to San Antonio, Texas. They had always loved to go to the movies together, so when they get together now that is what they do. And they don't stop with just one. They go for a movie marathon.

When I was young and single, I used to go up to Atlanta and do that. I think four in one day was my record, although with movies starting at noon you could probably squeeze in five if you really wanted to go all out. I know at my advanced age now I could never sit for that long. Nowadays, a couple in one day is my limit.

When Terry and I first married, I had to indoctrinate her into the ways of movie watching. She thought a movie was something you went to see every now and then—not every week, or a couple of times a week. But she soon became a good sport and joined in the pastime.

I think her patience and her back were tested when we lived in Rocky Mount, North Carolina. She was pregnant with J. J. at the time, and one Sunday afternoon I thought it would be great to ride from Rocky Mount to Raleigh and take in a movie. The problem was there were two movies playing I wanted to see, so she had to sit through them both. By the end of the second one she was really squirming. We didn't do that again.

Yes I am a movie fan, always have been and always will be. But I can't compete with those "four-movies-a-day" ladies. That time in my life is gone forever. But more power to them. I just wish I had known them was I was younger.

A Clue to Staying Young

In this cynical age in which we live, a lot of people would tell you marriage and fidelity are passé. I beg to differ. It is inspiring to note that many people get married and stay married. This point was driven home to me a few weeks ago when my wife Terry and I journeyed to St. Petersburg, Floriday, to help celebrate her parents' fiftieth wedding anniversary.

Terry had been working with her siblings on the party for weeks, and it all came off just fine. The honorees, the party givers, and the guests all seemed to enjoy the moment and some beautiful memories were made. Of course, it was also a time for some reflections on the past fifty years.

Terry had arranged a number of pictures that showed her mother and father through the years on a table, and looking at them I decided her mother has gotten prettier and prettier with age. Her dad still looks great, too.

The guests were all friends of her parents, and they were a lot of fun. One lady in particular was fascinating to me. She came up and asked, "Are you the one who does the movie thing?"

"I review movies," I answered.

"Well, have you seen *Fargo*?" she asked

When I replied that I had, she proceeded to tell me how much she loved it. Then she began to question me on every current movie in release and some of those to come. It seems she sees three to four a week every week—and she's eighty-one years old!

She admitted to me that she had always been a movie fan. Even when she was a little girl, if her parents wanted her to have a tooth pulled or she needed a shot for an illness or anything disagreeable, she would agree if they would promise to let her go to a movie soon afterward. As long as a movie was a part of the deal, she was fine.

Terry told me later that this woman is a widow who now spends her time traveling and going to movies and plays. The amazing thing is that she doesn't drive and instead takes a cab to each and every event if she doesn't have a friend who is going. Just this past month she had gone on a trip to London and had seen a total of nine plays in six days. Wow!

I don't know if going to movies and plays helped keep this woman young, but she sure didn't look like she was eighty-one. She had the look and enthusiasm of a much younger person. I guess keeping up with life and Hollywood kept her going.

That's the way I want to be when I grow up, just like this friend of Terry's parents. I want to be an eighty-one-year-old who stays interested in life. No rocking chair for me. I want to still be seeing a few movies a week and always anticipating the ones to come.

And like Terry's parents, I want to stay married to one person for fifty years. No, make that a hundred!

My Friend Earl

Earl Washington and his wife, Charlotte, are responsible for my wife Terry and me moving to Perry, Georgia. Now this may give them fame or infamy, but Earl and Charlotte are the people who invited us over from Warner Robins for supper one night and to visit their church, Perry United Methodist. That church became the reason for our move.

I had known Earl for several years at Robins Air Force Base, where we both worked. I was employed in the JAG office and he was in personnel. Although many, many people in Perry call him "Chip," I met him as Earl and that is the name I have kept for him.

Earl had a grand career at Robins before he retired a few years ago. Since that time he has stayed busy with working for Judge George Nunn and getting involved with several other projects. Chief among his activities is making people aware of the traits of Parkinson's disease, and being a fundraiser for research.

Earl himself was diagnosed as having Parkinson's back in 1993. To see and talk with him you wouldn't even be aware of this problem, but I know there must be times when it affects him a great deal. His outlook has remained upbeat and cheerful, but he is determined to do what he can to find help for himself and others with this disease.

In a few days there will be a statewide Parkinson's Disease Health Fair at the Georgia National Fairgrounds and Agricenter in Perry. The purpose of this meeting will be to educate people about this disease and some of the treatments available. One of the highlights of the day will be an appearance by Dr. Neil Shulman. This Emory cardiologist is the doctor/comic/author who reached national fame with his book *Doc Hollywood*. This book was made into a very popular motion picture starring Michael J. Fox.

Other persons involved in the battle to find a cure for this illness and to help people learn to live with Parkinson's disease will present information to the people attending. Even Attorney General Janet Reno, herself a Parkinson disease sufferer, has been invited to speak.

This "health fair" is a chance for people who have the disease to learn about treatments and other medical information. It is also a chance for all people concerned about and involved with Parkinson's disease to share their stories.

People who have this disease can lead productive lives. My friend Earl is an example of this. But we all need to do everything we can to help combat this illness. If we could do anything to help enhance my friend Earl's life, that would be enough for me. But if we could do something for the many, many people who suffer from this problem, it would be even better.

Mother's Day

"Mother's Day" is always a hard day for me. Well, in truth, all holidays of any sort are, but "Mother's Day" is particularly rough. I guess it is for anyone whose mother is deceased.

My mother died of cancer when I was fourteen. She was forty. At the time, I thought she had had a fairly long life. In retrospect I see that it had only just begun. Still, she managed to cram a lot of living into those forty years.

She was born Margaret Virginia Kershaw in Gadsden, Alabama. She was the youngest girl in a family of eight children. From pictures I have seen, she was beautiful from birth on. She was also headstrong and mischievous. My grandfather was not a wealthy man, but he had enough money to keep his family well provided for even during the Depression, and my mother enjoyed the benefits of upper middle-class living.

If there was anything my mother possessed it was a flair for the dramatic. My favorite story about her concerns her attendance at funerals. Her family home was located on a hill that overlooked a cemetery on the land below. Whenever my mother spied a funeral in progress she would rush from her house and join the mourners at the graveside. Legend has it that no one cried harder or moaned louder than she.

Her brothers and sisters nicknamed her "the buzzard" since she always was present at these sad events. But their taunts did little to dissuade her. When I asked her about it years later she told me that anyone who has died deserves to be mourned. She felt she was just doing her part.

My mother broke a lot of hearts in her day. She had multiple boyfriends who wooed her and asked for her hand. One of them had aspirations to be a college professor. When they broke up, he told her prophetically that one day he might teach her child. When my brother attended Furman University, this man was his English professor.

Every "Mother's Day" I am haunted by the memories of my mother's death, but for the most part my memories of her involve how she loved life. She had an enthusiasm for people and drew them to her. Our house was always full of people from the neighborhood or other parts of town who would come and sit and talk.

My mother loved to talk. In truth she loved to gossip. She was a storehouse of information about who, where, and what was going on in our small community. But she was never mean spirited with what she knew. She offered sympathy, encouragement, or advice—whatever was needed.

I have heard people say many times how their parents were their best friends, and most of the time I dismiss it. But in the case of my mother—during the short period of time that she was alive—she was my best friend. There was nothing about her I didn't like, nothing about her I didn't love. She was unique from anyone else I have ever known.

I never had a daughter on whom I could bestow her name. But I have high hopes for a granddaughter. If this child of the future is anything like Margaret Virginia "Gena" Cooper, she will be a special person indeed.

Mistaken Identity

Last weekend I was in New York again to see some movies and do some interviews. I had hoped to talk with Victor Browne while I was there, but it didn't work out. Victor is an actor from Warner Robins who is appearing on the daytime soap *One Life to Live*. I taped a segment last week to watch and spent the entire show thinking he was a certain character. When I saw the credits I learned it was someone else. Victor wasn't even on the show that day. Duhhh!

Anyway, I had a great time in New York. When I got ready to leave, the limousine picked me up, and it had a sign in the front window that said "Jackie Cooper" so I would know which one was mine. After I got in the car and we drove off, the driver left the sign in the window.

We stopped at a traffic light and a couple pulled up next to us on a motorbike. The woman looked over and hollered, "Is that the comedian Jackie Cooper?" The driver looked back at me, and I shook my head. He relayed the information to her that I wasn't the comedian.

"Are you sure?" she asked.

He looked back at me again, and I again said I wasn't.

"No," he told her.

By now we had moved down to a new traffic light.

"Roll down the back window and let me see," she demanded.

The driver looked back at me, and I nodded okay. He rolled the window down and she looked in and said "Say something to make me laugh."

I think I stuck my tongue out at her.

"I don't think that's funny," she said, and they took off.

I guess I made a bad impression for the comic Jackie Cooper, whoever he is. I never heard of a comedian by that name.

When we got to the airport the driver was getting my luggage out of the trunk. He turned to me and said, "Now I recognize you. You're famous."

"No, I'm not," I said.

"Yes, you are," he demanded, "and I know who you are."

I didn't even ask who I was. I just grabbed my bags and ran into the airport.

Once inside I heard someone yelling, "Tom Green, over here." I didn't react, and the same phrase was repeated.

Finally a very nice lady came over and tapped me on the shoulder.

"Mr. Green, our meeting is upstairs," she said, with a smile.

I told her I wasn't Tom Green, and I added it sure was a strange day since that was the third time someone had thought they recognized me as someone else. I pointed to the limo driver who was still outside and said even he had thought I was someone else.

"You know, he looks just like Tom Green's driver," she added with a mystified look on her face.

I never asked who Tom Green is. I just rushed back to Perry, Georgia, where I am who I am.

Holland Street

I was in South Carolina a few weeks ago for my stepmother's birthday celebration. While there I had a chance to visit with some of my friends from childhood, people who grew up on the same street as I did. As we talked, I realized what a charmed life we had back in the '50s and how special the neighborhood was on Holland Street.

All of my playmates lived on Holland Street or Stonewall Avenue, which intersected it. There were about fifteen of us of all ages, and for the most part we got along wonderfully. There were minor spats and disagreements, but on the whole, the kids of Holland Street stuck together.

We all walked to school together, and we all walked home together. Our parents never worried about our safety since we were such a large group. The older kids looked after the younger kids, and we all felt secure.

Summer was the most wonderful time on Holland Street. During the months of school vacation we all woke early and played late. We shot marbles, played dodgeball, went swimming, or did any of a hundred other things. When it was time for a meal, all our folks had to do was holler out the door and we would come running. Or we had sandwiches that had been packed so we could eat on the go.

During the summer we also undertook various projects such as "Sno-Jo" stands or rummage sales. My brother and I had the best Sno-Jo setup: a machine for scraping the ice for the cups. Then we added the various types of flavoring, and we were set. Customers came from far and wide.

At twilight, we would usually gather on the corner and tell ghost stories. As the sky grew darker, the mood of the evening would get scarier. There were many nights when I was waiting anxiously for my folks to call me home so I could escape that growing fear.

On Holland Street we had our share of deaths, divorces, and other dilemmas; but all my friends I have talked with who shared those days growing up say their memories are good. We lived in a world that was protected by our bond of friendship and the innocence of the time.

I worry that children growing up today are missing out on that kind of specialness. Still you can't miss what you have never had and most of them have never had a neighborhood group of that type. With the advent of air conditioning and the prevalence of television as entertainment, the desire to get together outside and congregate has diminished.

Holland Street is a world away now and its like may never be seen again.

Disney, New Orleans, and Me

The Disney Company knows how to do things right, and the marketing and selling of their new animated feature *The Hunchback of Notre Dame* is a prime example. To give the film a send-off-and-a-half the Disney folks gave a grand party in New Orleans and yours truly was invited.

I flew to New Orleans on a Monday which meant I had to bravely make my way up to Atlanta to catch my flight. I am one of those people who swore they wouldn't darken Atlanta's door until the Olympics were over. I have heard too much about the congested traffic and the fever pitch of all the activity there in preparation for the games. But you can't go anywhere in the South without starting, stopping, or changing in Atlanta. As one of my perceptive friends noted, when you die it doesn't matter if you are going to Heaven or Hell, you will still have to go through Atlanta.

So up to Atlanta I went and—surprise, surprise—the traffic wasn't bad and there were plenty of parking spaces at the airport. I had more than an hour to kill before my flight took off. That is when I became concerned about my money. I had not had time to get travelers checks, so I was carrying more cash than usual. I could just see me getting mugged in the airport and losing it all, so I decided to put it in my shoe.

That may not sound like such a bad idea except for the fact that I had on loafers and no socks. But put it in my right shoe I did, and then proceeded to walk with a limp. By the time I got to New Orleans, I had gotten used to the money being there, so walking from the gate where we landed to the transportation area didn't seem to bad. But as I walked, I felt something brushing against my ankle. At first, I didn't look but just thought it was a bug or something. It wasn't. When I finally did have the sense to see what was going on, I found I had a twenty-dollar bill sticking up out of my shoe. How that happened I'll never know, but I did manage to bend down and pluck it out without being obvious.

When I got to my hotel room, I vowed never to do that again. Not only did I risk losing all my money, but the bills had a distinctly "footy" smell to them. Still some things you have to try in order to learn they are a bad idea.

The hotel where I was staying was the headquarters for all the Disney troops, and believe me they were everywhere. Each was dressed in the essential Disney uniform: khaki shorts and a white T-shirt. On the day of a big party they threw at the Superdome, the T-shirts had become more colorful. There was green for the *event* sponsors, red for security, purple for maintenance, and white for the press chaperones. Folks, you had to see it to believe it. The amazing thing is that they all seem to know what they are doing.

On my first day there I had some free time so I decided to walk around the hotel and see a little bit of New Orleans. Well, I didn't see much. If you think Georgia is humid, think again. New Orleans has ten times as much moisture in the air and it's oppressive. I was outside for about an hour and it almost killed me. I made my way back to my air-conditioned room and didn't try any of that lengthy outdoor stuff again.

On Tuesday after I arrived, there was a press conference with a panel of vocal talents who had been associated with past and present Disney musicals. For example Jodi Benson was there since she was the voice of Ariel in *The Little Mermaid*. Paige O'Hara was also on board since she was the voice of Belle in *Beauty and the Beast*.

One of my favorite vocalists, Peabo Bryson, was there since he sang "A Whole New World" in the movie *Aladdin*. Peabo was asked about the Baptist boycott of Disney and he said he thought it was misguided. He said there are some much more serious problems in the world than Disney.

Judy Kuhn, the singing voice of Pocohontas was supposed to be there but she missed her connection in Atlanta and didn't arrive until the next day. Some poor soul asked a question of Jodi Benson thinking she was Judy Kuhn. He told her how much he had enjoyed her performance in *Sunset Boulevard* and wanted to know what she was doing next.

Jodi Benson is nothing if not cool. She answered that she was not Judy Kuhn and had not been in *Sunset Boulevard*, but if she had been she just knew she would have been marvelous. We all got a chuckle out of that, the guy who had made the mistake didn't feel so bad, and Jodi Benson showed what a class act she is.

The next day Disney staged a parade through the streets of New Orleans. The press had been given a spot right next to the parade route from which to view all the goings on. Even though it threatened to rain from time to time the sun held out and all the parade was seen without getting soggy.

It was a real New Orleans Mardi Gras-type parade with the various characters on the floats (Sleeping Beauty, Peter Pan, etc.) tossing out beads, crowns, and hand puppets to the crowd. Now, these beads are the type you could buy for next to nothing in any store, but you would have thought they were gold the way people were hollering for them.

It must be a crowd thing because even I yelled at poor Pocahontas to throw some beads my way. Hers got all caught up together and she couldn't get them separated so she tossed a clump of them my way. I just about had to step on a kid to get to them. I hope he wasn't hurt.

Later we all went to the Superdome where there was a stage show that the Disney Channel carried live. All of the musical voices we had at the press conference plus Judy Kuhn sang. It was really magical, especially when Lebo M and Carmen Twillery performed "The Circle of Life."

As Carmen and Lebo sang, they were joined by a group of dancers and a chorus. Just when you thought the stage was totally packed, out came four choirs from the side entrances, all singing their hearts out, and with a song that has such a strong meaning, this was the highlight of the night.

After the stage show was over, giant screens came down from the ceiling of the Super Dome and we all watched *The Hunchback of Notre Dame*. Then, there was a full fireworks display in the Dome. I mean they had fireworks going everywhere. I thought they were going to catch the roof on fire, but that Dome is high, high, high.

If you happen to catch the show on the Disney Channel in reruns, look for me. I am in section 141 and am the one wearing all the beads.

Long Distance Worry

A few weeks ago I called home to South Carolina to check on how my folks were doing. I was hoping they were feeling better than I was since I was fighting a sinus headache that had me popping pills. My stepmother Florence answered the phone and when I asked how she and my father were doing she replied, "We are the two most miserable people on the planet." My headache immediately moved up 500 notches on the pain scale.

She explained that she had fallen off the front porch steps a few days before. She had waited a day or so and then gone to the doctor. He said he thought she had broken a bone in her hip. The next day she was supposed to go to a bone specialist and get the results.

Bless her heart, at this point she didn't know if they would put her in the hospital or what. Daddy was on the extension crying and asking what was going to happen to them. He relies on her so heavily that he knew he couldn't survive if they put her in the hospital. I assured him I would come up and get him, if necessary, and bring him back to Perry with me. He didn't take that as reassurance.

The next day I called back and things were a little better. The doctor said she did have a clean fracture in her hip but they were not going to put her in the hospital. He didn't even want her to stay off of it completely. So she and Daddy were still in their home.

In Clinton, the church is the source of everything. People flocked to see them and brought food, offered rides to the doctor, offered to sit with Daddy, and a million other things.

Still, even with all this care I worried if they were safe and secure in their home. I still offered to bring them to Perry, but Florence said they would be alone all day since Terry and I work, and they would not know anyone. I knew this had to be their decision. I definitely do not want to impose my will on theirs just to make myself feel better.

After a few days Florence said she felt they were going to have to make some temporary move. She just couldn't care for Daddy and get well, too. So she and her minister started calling around and seeing if they could get in a retirement home on a temporary basis. Oddly enough, this is not easy to do. Most places want you full time or not at all—even if you can pay.

But they were lucky and did get into a retirement home. I went up to see them the day after they moved in. As nice as it was, it depressed me no end to see them there. First off, they were not in an apartment as I had thought. They were in rooms that resembled nice hospital rooms. It is called an "assisted care" room and has a medical staff on duty to give them medicine and care for them whenever needed.

Secondly, they were not in the same room. I thought they would be together instead of across the hall from each other. Florence probably will get more rest this way, but she still will have to go across the hall to check on Daddy which she does a lot.

Thirdly, they didn't have a phone or TV in their rooms. When I questioned this, she said they wouldn't be there long enough to justify getting them. It wasn't a money thing. It just wasn't practical. So I had to check on them by calling friends in Clinton rather than being able to talk with them directly.

As nice as the facility is, I worry about whether or not they are being truly taken care of. The people at the "home" look nice enough, but how do I really know what is happening. Being 200 miles away, I can't just drop in and check up on the care.

I read once that growing old is not for sissies. I agree. It takes courage, hope, and faith. I worry about my folks; I wonder if they are alright, and I pray that they are in good hands. That is what it all comes down to—what is best for the family. You worry and you wonder and you pray.

The Worry Continues

In the preceding story I told about my parents being in a retirement home. Well, now they are back in their own home. After a stay of only one week, they checked themselves out. For them, retirement home living was not what they thought it should be.

My stepmother called me and apologetically told me that she and Daddy were back in their house. She said the week they were at "the home" was miserable and she found herself getting more and more depressed. My father's medicine wasn't given on time; his bed was made up once while they were there; and the intercom squawked all night long. Plus, the food was of the institutional type and she just couldn't eat it.

Each day, she said, they sat in their rooms being miserable. Daddy finally began to sing "I want to go home" over and over. So home they went.

Luckily, they had entered this place on a day-by-day basis. If they had made the financial arrangement that a permanent stay would have entailed, they would have been stuck. But being day-by-day was costing them a very hefty sum of money and should have had provided them with better care.

Now, some may say that old people gripe about everything anyway and that is true of a lot of us regardless of our ages, but I believe in this situation the treatment and care of my parents was not what it was supposed to be. My stepmother sees things as they are and reacts to them accordingly, while my Daddy never has a bad word to say about anything. If it had just been him in this place, I probably would never have known the treatment was not up to par.

The question is, why wasn't the care better? Florence said there was a constant turnover in staff, which, to me, is a bad sign. She also said they had sick people mixed in with well, and that is depressing. And finally, she said the people who didn't have someone checking on them got the worst treatment.

Now don't take it that I am damning all retirement/ rehabilitation/nursing homes. I am not. I have friends in this business who I would trust with my life. But there are some rotten apples in the barrel. What we do to children and the elderly in this country is a crime.

If we're lucky, each of us is going to be old. Hopefully, we can pass through those final years with our dignity and our faith in our fellow human beings intact. In this instance with my parents and this facility, the experience was bad.

They are home now. The problem is not solved. Daddy still needs to be waited on and my stepmother shouldn't be trying to do it by herself. But she had been burned by this experience and doesn't want to be at anyone's mercy.

I am still calling. I am still worrying. I am still praying.

The Golden Rule

Good old-fashioned courtesy seems to have "gone with the wind" throughout the country. And when we do experience it, we seem shocked rather than expecting it. What happened?

When the Olympics were in Atlanta a few weeks ago the news media commented over and over again about how pleasant and courteous people were. They said they actually smiled at each other and stood in lines without shoving and pushing. But, they said, these are the Olympics, and they always bring out the best in people.

Sadly, that is probably true. Now that the Olympics have faded into memory, the screaming and horn blowing of drivers on the interstate, the shoving and surliness of the crowds at Lenox Mall, and the general sour attitude will become the rule of the day once more.

That is not to indicate that Atlanta is the mecca of moodiness. It is all around us. When was the last time you were in a store and the salesclerk actually seemed interested in waiting on you or helping you find something? How many times have you had someone keep you waiting while they visited with a friend or talked on the phone?

I was at the grocery store the other night and walked into a checkout lane. The woman standing at the cash register almost shrieked at me, "I'm closed!" Apparently, I had a lot of nerve coming into her lane when she was getting ready to go home. It sure would have been a heckuva lot nicer if she had said, "I'm sorry, sir, but I am closed. The person in the next lane will be glad to help you."

Then there was another example at a different grocery store a few nights later. At this one, I had an open lane to go through but the person checking me out could hardly scan the groceries. She was much more interested in talking to her boyfriend who stood behind her the whole time she was supposedly checking me out.

My wife says I am to blame for putting up with such rudeness and that I should always ask for the manager and report such lapses in behavior. But generally I am so disgusted that I don't want to do anything but get out of the store.

Plus, I could always take my business elsewhere, but I am a slave to convenience and don't want to go out of my way to make a purchase. So the rudeness and the sloppy behavior continue.

You know life would be so much easier if we all would remember the Golden Rule we learned as children. If we would do unto others as we would like them to do unto us, then we would all be courteous and polite.

In this age of answering machines, and instructions to hit "one" for such and such and "two" for something else, we all are desperate to talk to a human on the phone. So when we do get to talk with someone, or deal with them in person it sure would be nice to have it be a pleasant experience.

Life is too short and too hard to be faced with unnecessary unpleasantness. End of message. End of sermon. For now.

The Real World

One of my favorite programs on television is MTV's *Real World*. In case you haven't seen it, and I know many of you haven't, let me describe it to you. Seven young people, in their early twenties are moved in together in a house in a city and cameras are focused on them for a two- or three-month period.

This year the location of the "home" is in Miami. In previous shows it has been New York, Los Angeles, San Francisco, and even London. The group consists of three men and four women, and in this particular series of shows, the group has been challenged to start a business.

What fascinates me about this show is that these people let the cameras record their innermost thoughts as well as follow them around their house into all rooms—except the bathroom. We see them sleeping, eating, working and talking and talking and talking.

In most of the groups, one person has stood out as the troublesome one. In a few instances, the group has even banished one of the members from the home. Wouldn't that be awful? To be banished on national TV for failure to get along with the group?

I got to thinking about how it would be if the "real world" cameras invaded my home. Number one, I think all of my friends would stay away rather than be exposed to the glare of the camera. Secondly, I would have to learn to keep clothes on at all times rather than disrobing as soon as I walked in the door. And thirdly, I would have to watch my mouth and not make any snide remarks about anyone else.

So what else would you have? Well, the *Real World from Jackie Cooper's Home* would be boring television to the extreme. Even if I was willing to bare my soul on camera I have a wife who would kill me on the spot. I have learned over the years that there are things that sit well with her and things that don't. Any public revelations of this sort would be a definite no-no with her.

I don't even think my boys would get a kick out of it. We have all been too private with our world, and the people at MTV want controversy. They want to see fights and arguments and tragedy.

I do recall that a few years ago PBS did a similar program that looked at one family. They were named the Louds and they certainly were. That family had more infighting than I had every seen in my (then) young life. And after all the fighting was done and the show was over the parents got a divorce. I guess too much exposure can be a deadly thing.

But if you are ready, willing, and able to have the cameras turned on you, I think you should contact MTV about being in the next show. I think it would be great to watch *The Real World from Middle Georgia.* Just don't expect me and my family to drop by and participate. Well, I might come by, but I will leave my family at home.

Another World

When you turn on the TV these days you hear how you need to "come home" to CBS, or how "hot" the shows are on ABC, or how NBC has "must see" TV. That last one is the one that grabs me because for a large segment of my life TV was "must see." Now it has only become something I have time for when I don't have anything else to do.

Growing up in Clinton, South Carolina, I was a child when there was no TV. Or at least before it became common to every house in America. The first people I recall getting a television set were our neighbors John and Helen. When they got their set, it was a big event for the entire neighborhood.

John and Helen were a childless couple and spent a lot of time at home. The TV was a wonderful blessing for them as it occupied many long hours that might have otherwise been boring. Plus it was a draw to other neighbors to spend more time with them—especially the Coopers.

It seemed like we trekked across the street just about every night to watch some wonderful show. I know that we were always there on Wednesday nights to see *The Arthur Godfrey Show*. We talked about the people on that show like they were our best friends.

In the afternoons my mother and Helen loved to watch *This Is Your Life* and *Queen for a Day*. Both of these shows were tearjerkers, and the two ladies would cry bitter tears over the misfortunes of others. I would lay on the living room couch and watch through naps. Sometimes I might shed a tear or two over these poor souls, too.

When we finally got our own TV I felt like I was "King for a Day." To have it there, sitting in our living room and ready to be watched at anytime between 7:00 A.M. and midnight was an awesome power. I soon became a TV addict. Even when my then-girlfriend Elaine and I were dating, we would be at each other's house watching *American Bandstand* in the afternoon, or if we couldn't be together I would call her on the phone and we would watch from two houses but share the events.

In college there was a TV room in the dormitory basement and we would all congregate there for show after show. It got pretty raucous as we made comments about the people and plots we were watching. We had our own *Mystery Science Theater 3000* going long before the cult show was invented.

In law school we didn't have much time for TV, but somehow the soap *Another World* hooked us all, and in the afternoons between study sessions we tuned in religiously to see what was happening. We picked up legal tips from the TV murder trials and developed empathy for clients in the problems the different characters faced. The law school should have given credit for "Another World 101."

It was also in law school that I first knew someone who owned a color TV. The couple in the apartment next door to us had one, and my roommates and I visited them often to watch Johnny Carson at night. The husband loved having his "buddies" come over. The wife, I suspect in hindsight, wished we had had our own TV.

After I was out of school and married, I still watched a lot of TV. Terry loved *The Waltons* and we both liked *Bob Newhart* and *Mary Tyler Moore*. but when the boys arrived we cut down on our TV watching. There just weren't enough hours in the day.

Now TV holds little interest for me. The shows just don't seem as good as those that were offered years ago. I don't feel like I know these people and they sure aren't part of my family as were those nice Waltons, or Mary or Bob.

NBC can say they are offering "must see TV" but somehow the message just isn't getting through to me.

A Kiss Is Just a Kiss

Does the song refrain "You must remember this, a kiss is just a kiss…" echo in your mind as you look at the picture of the six-year-old boy who was suspended from school for kissing a six-year-old girl on the cheek? Somebody should play it for the school board that supported his suspension.

Where is all this political correctness going to lead? What must have started as well-intentioned actions have now dissolved into ludicrous and hypocritical behavior. And this six-year-old's kiss is the height of ridiculousness.

When I was child we played spin the bottle at parties. Do they still do that anywhere? Probably not. But back then the boys and girls would sit in a circle and spin a milk bottle or soft drink bottle and whoever of the opposite sex it would point to would get a kiss. Usually the discrete couple would go into the next room for the momentous event.

Would that be sexual harassment today? Well, it could be construed as that. I ended up kissing a lot of girls I didn't want to and I am sure a few received my well-intentioned offering with less than anticipation. But it was all part of the game—and a game was all it was.

I always thought sexual harassment had to be an act that intimidated another, or was some act that was imposed on another person against his or her will. If both participants are willing, how can it be harassment? Or can society say what constitutes harassment without taking into consideration what the two involved parties think?

I know that everyone thinks their childhood was a time of innocence, but I really do think that the '50s were the last great heyday for unlocked doors and safe streets—and sanity. I honestly knew nothing about drugs until I was grown and was working as an investigator for the Air Force. Some of my friends drank in high school, but it was never the get-drunk-fall-down thing.

My best friend Alice smoked like there was no tomorrow and was the one who got me started. We would sit on the curb on the street behind her house and puff away. She could French inhale and blow smoke rings, so she was a super smoker. I guess I was so impressed by her smoking prowess that I at least had to light up.

Me, I was a smoke-and-cough smoker. Plus I was totally naïve. I actually thought I could smoke in my room with the window open and my folks would never have a clue. Boy, does that sound dumb. The funny thing was that my father never confronted me on it until I was in my freshman year of college. One weekend he was driving me back to school and as I got out of the car he tossed me one of those free samples of cigarettes they used to hand out. "Maybe you want these," he said.

But back to Alice. Alice taught me to smoke, told me how to act to attract girls, and generally ran my life for a few years. Was I harassed? You bet! Was it actionable? Never in a million years. And, come to think of it, I think I kissed her on the cheek several times when some of her advice had paid off for me.

I guess I could have been suspended from school. Me and the six-year-old suspended for random kissing.

Is There a Doctor in the House?

Just a few days ago I was at work at my office in Macon, Georgia, and as things turned out, I thought I was going to have to deliver a baby. In the words of the immortal Prissy, "I don't know nothing' about birthin' no babies." Luckily the situation didn't get quite that far—but it almost did.

The day started innocently enough. My crew and I were our usual busy selves at my office. The only out-of-the-ordinary thing was that the phone repairman was working in the back room on the phone lines. Then out of the blue, everything changed.

Mary, a lady who works with me, asked if I could catch the phone as she was not feeling too good. Since she was eight months pregnant I wasn't surprised that she wasn't feeling her best. So I assured her I would, and then forgot about her feeling bad. But a few minutes later Paula, another lady in the office, came running down the hall hollering. "Call 911. Mary needs an ambulance."

Now I pride myself on being calm under fire. When both my boys were born, I stayed relatively sane during the drive to the hospital and the ensuing excitement. Plus, I had always made fun of the people who screamed into the phone on that *911* show. So it was with surprise that I found myself screaming at some poor schmuck who answered the 911 line that I needed an ambulance and fast!

"I'll connect you with the emergency room," he said, quickly, and in a moment I heard a voice announcing it was the emergency room. But when I started giving details about who I was what I needed, they said they were the Air Force base hospital and couldn't come to Macon.

"Why did they give me you?" I shouted.

"I don't know," she answered.

"Well, get him back," I demanded, and she did.

"Wait a minute and I'll connect you with the right place," he promised. And in a few minutes he had me connected—with the Houston County Hospital thirty minutes away! And again I went through my story after which they told me they couldn't come to Macon.

A second call to 911 revealed the problem. Even though my office is in Macon, it has Robins AFB phones. So I was getting the Houston County 911 service. But this explanation didn't satisfy me. I said he had to get me through to Bibb County 911. He said he would have to call the sheriff's office, and he would have to look up the number.

In the meantime, it sounded like we were getting closer to a baby. I was getting minute by minute reports from the people who were attending Mary. One lady suggested we just bundle her up and take her in a car, but I had seen too many movies where the car gets stuck in traffic and the baby won't wait. I vetoed the idea.

I kept wondering how we might boil water. You always have to have boiling water, don't you? And crazily I kept hearing over and over in my mind that famous statement of Prissy's in *Gone with the Wind*. It was something like "My mama told me that if you put a knife under the bed it cuts the pain." I think that was about the time Scarlet slapped her.

As we waited for the ambulance to arrive, the phones were ringing off the hook. One guy who calls me often from another base for information usually uses a famous name. In the past, he's used Tom Cruise, Kevin Costner, and Cecil B. DeMille. In the middle of this chaos, my secretary called me and said that Boris Karloff was on the line. For a moment my fevered brain actually thought it might be him.

Finally the ambulance arrived. As the paramedics left the building, the phone man stepped from the storeroom and announced, "I got the static out of your phone line." He never mentioned our medical emergency at all. Maybe he was so focused he didn't hear a thing.

That night Mary had a fine baby boy and I am pleased to tell you mother and son are fine. I guess she had a pretty good doctor. I am sure he did a better job than I could have done. Or maybe not!

Whoop, Whoop, Whoopeee!

It was a match made in heaven: Whoopi and the Whoopee. Actress Whoopi Goldberg has a new movie out called *The Associate*. Macon has a new hockey team called the Whoopee. Could one endorse the other? Does ice melt in the summer?

Rumors flew that Whoopi herself would come South for the first home game of the Whoopee, but that was not to be. Instead she autographed the first puck used in the game. Isn't that special! And with that blessing from the Whoop the team skated to a win.

How do I know all of this? Well, I was there for the opening night game. Dave Tribble of the Michael Parver Agency in Atlanta represents Disney for events in Georgia and other states. He was the one who got Whoopi to sign the puck since *The Associate* is from Disney's Hollywood Pictures. Dave got the autograph and a ton of publicity for the team, and team manager Pat Nugent sent him some tickets for the first game.

Funny about that Pat Nugent name. Wasn't somebody named that married to Lucy Baines Johnson? Just asking. Having my celebrity name, I am always curious about others so afflicted.

Anyway, Dave called and said he had an extra hockey ticket. My first thought was "So?". Then I realized he meant he had one for me. I was not overjoyed at the prospect of going to a hockey game, even one in Macon. My son the sportswriter thought it was a neat opportunity, but I was thinking of the movie I would have to forego in order to cheer on the team.

But Dave is a good friend, and after all, I had seen all three Mighty Ducks movies. I knew a little about hockey from those viewings, so off I went.

I have to say I enjoyed it. Dave said hockey is always a fast sport, but this one absolutely flew by. The puck was going everywhere and the players were keeping up with it without a problem. Even the referees were good enough for the Ice Follies. I later had someone tell me the referees were players whose careers did not take off.

What was even more exciting were the slam-bam fights out there on the ice. People got slammed into the plastic walls and the crowd went wild. It is more like wrestling than any other sport I have ever seen.

I was just as amazed at how the crowed had already developed cheers and dances—and this was the first home game. A group of men behind us yelled, "Whoop, whoop, Whoopees" in unison over and over. A slightly fragmented wave swept around the arena. And one lovely young lady had a victory dance that defies description. Every time the Whoopee scored, she graced us with this rhythmic sway-along.

Now, am I going to be at every Whoopee game from now on? I don't think so. But I did have a good time, and you should try it too. Whether hockey will make a go of it in our area is yet to be seen, but on a nice October night, with the Whoopi puck on the ice, the excitement and thrill of the game got to me.

Whoop, whoop, whoopeeeeee!

Who the Heck Is Peter Boyle?

A few years ago I was out in Hollywood interviewing James Earl Jones. He was the voice of Mufasa in the Disney animated movie *The Lion King*. While I was talking with him, he stopped our conversation to say I looked just like one of his best friends. As the conversation continued, he kept going back to the fact that I was the very image of this good friend who is an actor.

I had visions in my head that it must be Harrison Ford, Mel Gibson, or even Jack Nicholson, but it wasn't. It seems he thinks I am the spitting image of Peter Boyle. Boyle is an actor who rose to fame in a movie called *Joe*. He later gained renown as Frankenstein's monster in the Mel Brooks movie *Young Frankenstein*. Do you catch my drift? I was not thrilled with the comparison.

Fast forward to the present. Last week I began taping entertainment reports that will air on one of the local TV stations. For the first report, I had an interview with Garry Marshall, the director of the new movie *Dear God*. The interview was taped, but I appeared live to introduce the interview and to say a few words afterwards.

Television is not a new medium for me. I have been doing various shows for the past few years. On these shows, however, I was the guest and the brunt of the responsibility for how I did fell on someone else. They would ask me questions about the entertainment world and I would respond with a short quip or two.

On this new show I am the one in charge. I have to fill up two to three minutes and I have to make sure it flows interestingly. Even though I had a guest in this case, I still had to do the introduction and the exit.

I felt a little strained doing the show and hoped it didn't show. When I got a chance to look at the segment (I had taped it) I realized I looked nervous and tired and goofy. My eyes were wandering around like squirrels looking for acorns. The only blessing was they weren't going in different directions.

At first I was looking at the monitor, then I was looking at the wrong camera, and then I was grinning like a toothless wonder. My eyes had bags under them that would have held clothes for a two-month vacation. My hair, which always is there when I look in the mirror had somehow faded away to leave a bald spot the size of Asia. Plus, God gave me one chin, but somehow I have added three to his gift.

Oh, and one last thing. I looked exactly like Peter Boyle.

The Buzzard Was My Mother, Not Me

I have confessed it before and now I do so again: my mother was nicknamed "the buzzard" because as a child she would go to the cemetery near her home and join in the mourning of complete strangers. That love of funerals did not pass down to me. The love of morbidity maybe, but not the love for the funeral itself.

In fact, I usually avoid funerals at all costs and can count on one hand those that I have attended. But I did go to one recently. It was for the husband of one of the ladies in my Sunday school class.

This was not your usual funeral, or at least not in my book. To start with, the entire service took place at the graveside. There was no preacher to lead the service, but the funeral director did read some scripture. Then several people stood up and talked about the dearly departed. Even the widow had a few words to say.

The unique thing about all this was that a lot of the stories about the deceased were humorous. At first people hesitated to laugh, but finally decided it was okay. Even the stories told by the widow were upbeat and funny.

If there was anything I have ever attended which was close to an Irish wake, well, this was it. It was informal, sad, funny, and informative. I had not really known the man who died, but by the time the service was over I thought I knew him fairly well. And I had several different perspectives of him.

In truth, I was one of the people who spoke at the graveside service. I followed right behind the funeral director. My wife was horrified that I did not have a printed talk to give, but I decided that since I hadn't known the person who died that well, I would just wing it. I figured God would tell me what to say.

What I ended up doing was talking about him through his wife. I related how she had told me her husband's opinions on many things when we would talk in Sunday school (He did not attend.). I also shared how proud he seemed to be of her on the few occasions when I was around him. He would glow with pride as she participated in various events.

And for her part, she seemed to be completely devoted to him. He seemed to inspire her love and her respect. They were married for twenty-two years, so something had to be right.

It just seems that sometimes God let's us get a glimpse of Heaven through those we love. We see it in their faces and in their actions. I think that was the case with this couple. He got a glimpse of Heaven through his wife's love.

I hope my brief talk added something valuable to the service. It was meant from the heart. I know I enjoyed the words of the other speakers. They appeared to be sincere and spoke with deep affection. When I go I only hope as many people can say nice things about me. And I guess that is one funeral I will have to attend.

Don't Get on My Bad Side

Celebrities and their quirky ways always amaze me. Now on the whole, I have to say my dealings with "stars" have been positive, and my recent encounters with Shirley MacLaine and Marion Ross were no exception. But they did show a little bit of vanity that was above and beyond the norm.

I went to Atlanta to interview the two ladies for their upcoming film *The Evening Star*. This is the sequel to the mega-successful *Terms of Endearment*. Shirley once again plays Aurora Greenway and Ross is cast as her maid Rosie.

I saw the movie on Monday night and had the interviews the next day. My interview with Ross was scheduled for 8:30 A.M. and I was the first person talking with her. This was a TV interview so they had to have the lights set up and the mikes in place.

I went to the chair where the TV people told me to sit and Marion Ross sat opposite me. She was very pleasant and told me that she had visited Perry and Hawkinsville in the past. By then, the TV people said we were ready to start. But just before they said, "Roll 'em," she turned to me and said, "Is this my good side?"

She was pointing to the left side of her face. I didn't know how to respond. I said something inane like it looked fine to me. Then she repeated, "But do you think this is my best side?"

I just sat there saying nothing as she muttered to herself, "I will be turned this way talking and I don't think this is my best side."

She looked up and asked, "Would you swap seats with me?"

I answered that was up to the TV crew since they had put us the way they wanted us. She repeated the request to them and they said okay. So off came the mikes and changes were made to the lights. Then we went on with the interview and everything was fine.

My interview with MacLaine was scheduled for 10:30 that morning. At 10:15 I went to the room where we were to wait for our interviews to start. When I got there, there were three other people in the room. One was a guy from CNN, the next was a woman from Nashville and the third was a man from Chattanooga.

In talking with them I learned the CNN interview was supposed to have been at 10; the Nashville one at 10:10; and the Chattanooga one at 10:20. None of them had happened. Things were getting a little backed up.

At 10:30 the public relations person handling the interviews came and told us there was a slight problem. At 10:40 she came back and said the problem was taking a little longer than expected. Finally, at 10:50 the interviews started.

It seems Shirley did not like the lighting at all when she sat down in the chair and the crew had to get it all done to suit her. Strangely, when I got to the room to interview her (which was the same place I had interviewed Ross), the lighting looked just the same.

At least she didn't ask about her good side and was sitting firmly in the chair where Ross had started out. In my opinion she looked years younger than sixty-two, so maybe the lighting worked after all. I'll just have to wait and see how I looked under the MacLaine lighting.

But good side and good lighting aside, this hassle from the stars almost got them on my bad side and nobody wants to do that! Grrrr!

The Grinch Is Back, One More Time

Once again this year, I am having a hard time getting into the Christmas spirit. It's too hot and the world seems too ordinary. I have been to the malls, but rather than putting me into the giving spirit they have made me crankier than usual.

First off, let me say I am the world's worst shopper. Just ask my wife. For a second opinion, ask my kids. If I know something definite I wish to purchase, I go to the store, go right to the spot where it is, and buy it. None of this going up and down the aisles for me.

The other night, my wife talked me into going to the mall. It was not a great experience. At the first store we bought a camera. Rather than being able to get the gift right there, we were sent to the underground receiving station. There were a lot of people ahead of us.

This store had one guy getting packages for people. It wasn't that he was slow but that he was overworked. You would think that at Christmas they could hire some extra help. If there was any extra help around, they were all on break.

After we finally got our package there, we went shopping for other gifts. We found a sweater for my stepmother at a department store. When we paid for it we asked for a box to put it in. We were told we would have to go to gift wrapping to get one. When I tried to explain that we didn't want it gift wrapped but only wanted a box to put it in, I was told that it didn't matter.

It seems the people who are supposed to keep boxes supplied at the cash registers hadn't replenished the stock—not there or at any of the other locations in the store. So down to the basement we went where we had to take a number and wait. Once again, there were a lot of people ahead of us.

As we were leaving the store, I saw an item I needed to buy for one of my co-workers, but there was no box at the register to put it in. When I was told I would have to go back to gift-wrapping I said thanks but no thanks. That is one less sale that store will make, but from the attitude of all involved, who cares!

I have said it a million times but no one listens. What has happened to people appreciating your business? In this age of downsizing and people losing jobs, you would think courtesy would be more alive and well than ever.

There was a grocery store I used to patronize. It was close and convenient and that's why I used it. But, as a whole, the people who worked there were the rudest bunch you could ever ask for at any time. No matter what lane you got in or what service you needed, it was a drain on whoever was waiting on you.

Guess what? That store is now out of business. I wonder if the people who were so lackadaisical about their customers feel differently now. I hate to say it, but I doubt it.

Now, before I become the total grinch, let me say that before Christmas arrives I will get a better attitude. And when I am out shopping on Christmas Eve, as I inevitably am, I will probably get a feeling of oneness with other shoppers. And before Santa Claus comes down the chimney I will get a sense of the real meaning of Christmas and count my blessings.

So to all of you and yours, a merry Christmas and a joyous holiday season.

Chapter 2

Reflections from Route 97

Life Is Good

When Christmas arrives it brings with it all the joys of the season, but it also means for me and my wife that we will get a few days off at Jekyll Island, Georgia. For years now, we have set aside the days immediately following Christmas as time for us. And that time is spent with rest and recuperation at Jekyll.

In past years our two boys have gone with us, but when they are twenty-one and twenty-four, they have their own agenda. Maybe after they're married and have families of their own, they may get back in the Jekyll mood, but for now it's "no way."

We have also been joined by friends and other family members from time to time, but the truth of it is we are just too boring when we go. Nobody wants to spend time just watching videos and reading. Hey, it works for me.

My wife does sometimes walk on the beach while we are there. And I do like to hear the ocean. I open up the doors to our room and turn the heat on high and let the surf boom to its heart's content. There is nothing so soothing as the sound of the surf.

I always like to arrive at Jekyll late in the afternoon or in the early evening, preferably when it is dark, so people won't gape when they see me unpacking my VCR and my electric fan. People tend to think when you have a VCR at a motel you are going to be watching dirty movies, and they don't know what to think about the fan. I guess they imagine it's some kind of fetish.

Well, my fan goes everywhere with me. The sound of the surf may be soothing but I can't sleep without the sound of my fan. I turn it on as soon as I get to my room and turn it off only when we are packing up to leave.

The second thing I do (after turning on my fan) is hook up the VCR. This year we took about a dozen videos with us and I watched six of them in a three-day span. Some of the Hollywood studios had sent me screening copies of their year-end releases, so I got to preview *Shine, Everyone Says I Love You, The English Patient*, and three other preview tapes. It was a moviefest and I loved it.

Our trip to Jekyll always follows a routine. The first day we arrive is our transition from work. It takes about a day to get your mind out of the "what I ought to be doing" mode. Then the next two days are pure relaxation. The fourth day is the "I don't want to go back" day, full of longing to stay at the beach and resentment at having to start work again.

The amazing thing about Jekyll is that it cleanses the mind and soul. Everyone needs a place where they can go and escape the worries of the day. It may just be a room in your house, or a spot in your yard, but everyone needs such a place.

My problem is that now that the vacation is over, I have to wait for the next one. But anticipation is half the fun. I enjoy thinking about going, I enjoy being there, and when I return I enjoy thinking about the next time.

Life is good.

Remember Sean, Forget Terry

Anyone who knows my wife knows she has a horror of going to the dentist. Just going to have her teeth cleaned is enough to get her quaking in her shoes. I, on the other hand, think nothing of getting teeth filled or extracted.

I have heard horror stories from people about dental experiences, most of which centered around having wisdom teeth pulled. That is one thing I never have to worry about as I have never had wisdom teeth. Just call me stupid, but for some evolutionary reason they never appeared in my mouth.

My wife did, though, and shortly after we were married, she had to have them extracted. I don't know exactly how long we had been married but I remember thinking it was going to be one of those tragic love stories where the wife dies within months of the marriage.

She had a terrible time and developed what is known as a "dry socket," and it was terribly painful for her. The dentist prescribed some morphine tablets and that made matters worse. My wife is allergic to morphine.

We got through it, but it was not a good experience. Therefore, we were apprehensive when we discovered that our younger son had to have his four wisdom teeth removed.

My wife Terry made arrangements to be off that day so that she and my son's fiancée, Paula, accompanied him to the dentist's office. Oh yes, I forgot to add that the surgery was scheduled for Christmas Eve.

Sean, Terry, and Paula arrived at the dentist's office a little before 8:00 A.M. When I hadn't gotten a call by 10:00 A.M., I called the office. The people there explained that he hadn't actually had the surgery yet, but it would start at any time.

I think this overprotective attitude drove Paula crazy, but that's the way we are in this family. I say this because she told me later that Terry kept asking how things were going from the time Sean went into the dentist's office.

The amazing thing is how good everything went for Sean. He came out of the dentist's office and went home where he slept most of the afternoon away. But by that night he was out with Paula celebrating Christmas, and even later that evening he came over to our friend's house where we were visiting.

Sean says the reason he did so well is because he wasn't put to sleep when he had it done. Of course it also made a difference that his teeth weren't imbedded in bone.

So, there is hope for those of you who are facing having your wisdom teeth removed. Remember Sean had it done and it was easy. Oh, and forget about Terry and her dry socket and her reaction to morphine. We want to think positive here.

The Attack of the Vending Machine

Do you ever feel that the simplest things you do have a tendency to turn into the most complicated? Take, for instance, the act of buying a paper out of a vending machine. Sounds simple, doesn't it? Well, not for me. The other night when I was coming home from work I decided I wanted to read the local newspaper. We get a copy at home but usually my wife takes it with her to work and I never get a chance to see it.

When I got the machine opened all the papers except the one in the display case had been sold. And for some reason the one in the rack portion did not want to come out. I had to pull and tug to get it loose. As I got it loose, the open slot shut and caught my coat jacket in it. Now I had a paper but I couldn't get my coat loose.

In a situation like this, you do not have your sharpest thoughts. I honestly wondered to myself if I was going to have to pull the vending machine over to my car in order to get 50 more cents to reopen the rack. But then it dawned on me—duh! I could take off my coat, go to my car, get the money and then come back. Luckily I had fifty cents in change in my car. When I got my coat back, a couple in a car drove up. They said they had been watching the whole thing from across the street. They were almost doubled over with laughter and said if they had had a video camera I would have won them a heap of money on *America's Funniest Videos.*

This instance reminded me of a similar event in my childhood. As a child I loved to climb trees. Now, to this day I have a fear of heights and did then, I think, but I still liked to make my way to the topmost branches. One day I was up the street at my friend Nancy's house. She and I were out in her yard and I decided to climb one of her trees. I quickly made it to a suitable distance and hollered down for her to look at me.

While showing off I lost my grip on the limb on which I was sitting and began to fall. I managed to grab hold with my legs and slipped down to the "vee" of the limb, and that is where I stuck. You get the picture, don't you? I was upside down hanging from the tree by my leg. Nancy was laughing so hard she wasn't any help at all, but finally she got herself composed and got some help.

The guy who came to help me down said he thought they would have to saw my leg off, since it was so wedged in the tree. He was being funny, but I thought he was serious. When he got the saw, I guess my face tuning up to cry made him confess that he was only cutting the branch.

I got down finally and I swore off climbing trees forever. How was I to know that trees, newspaper vending machines, and so on, would be attacking me all the rest of my life. Maybe my life is just one continuous episode of *America's Funniest Videos.*

My Father, My Son

I am constantly amazed by how much my son Sean is like my father. It can't be from association because my father lives in South Carolina, and aside from occasional visits has not been a major part of my sons' lives. But every year I see more and more traits of my father in my younger son.

To start with, they are two of the most likeable people in the world. Everybody who meets Sean loves him, and everyone who has ever had contact with my father feels the same way. I remember when my mother was alive she told me once that she had never heard my father say he really disliked anyone, and that there probably wasn't anyone who really disliked my father.

He has always been the one who gets along with everyone in the family, and that is a monumental task: we are a family of high tempers and long grudges. My mother was one who could flare up quickly and she was forever involved in spats with my aunt who lived in the same town as we did.

The only person my father has ever told me he didn't like was his father. My grandfather was a mean, cold man who made my father's life miserable. My mother despised him. My father just said he didn't like him much.

Another trait Sean and my father have in common is a love of sports. My daddy loved to play softball, and of course so does Sean. I can remember my mother taking my brother and me to the ball field on warm summer nights to watch Daddy play. Most of the time my brother and I would wander off to play with the other kids, but those times when I did watch my daddy, he did great.

And when he would come over to us after the game, he always had that sweet and sour smell that comes with playing hard. I loved that smell and do to this day. When my father would hoist me up on his shoulders to walk us home I would get his smell on me and I thought that made me really big.

I can't say that Sean smells like my daddy, but he does have his form on the softball field. He is a natural athlete and thoroughly enjoys playing the game. Like my daddy, he is a big man and has a lot of power.

This summer when Sean gets married, my Daddy is planning to attend. He says that is what he is living for, and in a way that is true. He has a goal to reach and I am betting on him to do it. I sure do hope he can come because Sean is counting on it. He needs his "twin" to be there for him on that special day.

Living in the Now

Recently I was listening to a commentator on the radio. I don't even know who it was, but something he said really hit home with me. He said, "Yesterday is gone; tomorrow is a promise; and today is a gift—that's why they call it the present."

I think all of us spend too much time living in the past or the future and not enough in the today. At least that has been my way a lot of the time. When I was younger I dreamed about being able to drive, being on my own, being in the future. Now that I am older, I spend a lot of my time thinking about what used to be.

There was never a time when I thought this is the now I have been wanting. And there should have been such a time. I guess if I had to pick the most perfect "now" it would have been when my boys were small. From the day they were born, they were a joy and they have continued to be so.

I look at pictures now and I see them as babies and then as toddlers and then as school age, and I wonder where it all went. All I know is that it flew by. When I hear parents wish their kids were older, I want to grab them and shake them and tell them to hold on to what they have because it all goes so fast.

Still, even with my kids grown up I am trying to stay in the now and not in the past. And there is a lot to be said for being a couple on their own again. If on a Sunday afternoon we want to go to a movie there are no arrangements that have to be made; we just do it.

And when the lure of Jekyll Island grows great we don't have to coordinate schedules with anyone. We just pack up the car and go.

And if I want to watch a certain television show there is no conflict. We have two TVs and that's enough for me and my wife each to see what we want.

Boys, movies and TV shows, and freedom; I would trade it all in a flash to be obligated to caring for my kids again. Maybe the future grandchildren will need me. There I go living in the future again. I guess some things can't be changed.

There's No Place Like Home

One of the things my wife said to me when we were first married was "Never make me live in a small town!" This was understandable since she had lived in St. Petersburg, Florida, most of her life and was used to big-city living. So I promised her I never would.

The first year of our marriage was spent in Warner Robins since I was in the Air Force at the time. When I was discharged, we went to Rocky Mount, North Carolina, which is a moderate-sized town. We only stayed there a year and then moved back to Warner Robins.

We were never happy in Warner Robins. That is not a put-down of the city or the people who live there. Somehow we just couldn't make the right connections with a church or a neighborhood. As soon as we would get to know a couple we felt we could be close friends with, they would up and move. Maybe it was us, but for whatever reason we were just not happy.

One day a friend I was working with invited Terry and me to have supper with him and his wife. They lived in Perry. As we drove into the town I began to feel at home. It had the same look and feel to it that my hometown of Clinton, South Carolina, has.

After supper, it being a Sunday, we went to church with our hosts. They attended the Perry United Methodist Church.

Even though I had been raised Baptist (through and through, dyed in the wool) I felt like this, too, was a homecoming.

The next Sunday, Terry and I drove from Warner Robins to Perry for church services and we continued to do so for the next several weeks. Finally, we decided if we were going to be active in the church we might as well move to Perry. I asked Terry if she though she could be happy there, and she said she would give it a try.

We contacted a realtor and she showed us several houses, none of which fit our fancy. But one day she called and said she had found our house. She just knew that it was perfect and it was. As soon as I walked in the door, I knew it was right. It reminded me of the house I had gown up in Clinton.

We lived in that house for seven or eight years. Then I was offered a job in California. I had always wanted to live in California, so I was raring to go. Terry wasn't as enthusiastic. She didn't want to leave Perry and her small-town lifestyle. But being a supportive wife, she agreed and off we went.

We were only in California for two years when we had the chance to come back to Georgia. Terry and the boys were more than happy to come back. I was a little more reluctant. But being a supportive husband, it was my turn to agree.

We came back to Perry in November 1982. As we pulled off the interstate and drove down Sam Nunn Boulevard, the warm feelings of the town flooded over me. I was home. And when we went to church on Sunday, the return was complete. In the blink of an eye our stay in California had become a memory.

Songwriters and poets have talked for ages about what home really is. To my family and me, it is Perry. I know it would not necessarily be the place for everybody, but wherever your place is, I hope you find it soon. It is true that "there is no place like home" and when you have found it, you know it.

That's What Friends Are For

A few months ago I delivered a funeral eulogy for the first time in my life. That was quite an experience. Now I have had a new chapter to add. I have gone from funeral eulogist to funeral soloist.

Ten to fifteen years ago, my friend Alice told me her mother was ill. For some unknown reason, Alice then asked me if I would sing at her mother's funeral. Being younger and being possessed of a pleasant, if not tremendous voice, I said yes. But Alice's mother recovered and I thought the moment had passed.

Now flash forward to the present. I'm at work and the phone rings. It's Jackson, Alice's son. He tells me that his grandmother is very sick and that Alice wants to remind me of my promise to sing at the funeral. I sputtered something to Jackson about my voice being a thing of the past, but he just laughed and said he was sure I would do fine.

That night I prayed for Alice's mother's recovery—for her good and mine. But God had decided to call her home, and the next day at work I got a call from Alice: "Jackie, I need you to come and sing."

That night the funeral director that was handling the arrangements for the ceremony called. "Mr. Cooper, I understand you will be doing two songs at the funeral," she said.

"I am?" I answered.

"Will you be bringing your accompanist?"

I answered, "No."

"Oh, you play for yourself?"

"No!" (Didn't this woman understand I never got past "Here we go up a row, to a birthday party?")

"I guess you will want to meet with the church organist then?"

"Oh, yes!"

The next day, when I met with Alice I told her I had decided to sing "Softly and Tenderly" and "The Old Rugged Cross." She said that was fine, but she really wished I would sing "Beyond the Sunset" since they had sung that at her father's funeral.

I explained that I didn't know "Beyond the Sunset" so I couldn't sing it. She said she understood, but she really, really wished I would sing it. So what do you do? At two o'clock the organist taught me "Beyond the Sunset."

In the order of service, there were to be three ministers and me. One would pray, then I would sing; then the second would pray, and I would sing again; and then the third minister would make the comments about the deceased.

The first song I sang was "The Old Rugged Cross." As I sang it I saw a few faces of people I knew. They looked like they were thinking, "What in the world is Jackie Cooper doing standing up to sing?!"

By the time I stood up for "Beyond the Sunset" they were used to me being there. The look on Alice's face as I sang this song made all the fear and trembling I had gone through worth it.

I have told people about this incident and they all ask me why in the world I agreed to sing. The answer is simple: Alice asked me. She is my friend and when friends call on you, you say yes. If you don't, then what is friendship for?

The Mist of Memory

Do you remember that "The Reader's Digest" used to have a section called "The Most Unforgettable Person I Ever Met"? They may still have that feature, but I haven't seen it in a long time. Anyway, the other day I was thinking about some of the "unforgettable" people I have known and one name immediately stood out in my mind. Her name is Joan Chase.

For several years, Joan ran the Perry Bookstore. But ultimately, she sold it and headed up north, where I guess she still is. One bad thing about "unforgettable" people is that you sometimes tend to lose touch with them.

When Joan first opened the Perry Bookstore, I had not yet met her, but being a lover of books and bookstores in particular, I ambled in and made her acquaintance. Joan was one of those people you feel like you have known for years even when you have only known them for a few minutes. Ten minutes and we were buddies.

While Joan operated the bookstore, it never had a wide selection of books. It was certainly no B. Dalton's or Waldenbooks. Joan, however, would locate any book you wanted, and more importantly, she would recommend books she knew you would like.

Many afternoons I would leave work, and before I would head home, I would stop by and visit with Joan at the bookstore. In winter, she had a fire going and in summer the bright sunlight illuminated the store. I liked the wintertime best and could sit on the fireplace edge and talk and drink coffee until all the pains of the day had fled.

It was Joan who talked me into reviewing books, which I do to this day. She simply said that anyone who loved books like I did should tell people about them. She also told me to slap my name on some letterhead and book companies would send me review copies by the tons. So I did, and so they did. My house became a virtual library.

Joan was also business smart. She told me that any business had to have a gimmick, something that would make it stand out. By accident she found hers for the bookstore. It came in the shape of a kitten that was at her door one morning when she opened up. The kitten found a warm place in the sun and promptly went to sleep. It woke only for food and affection. The rest of the time it slept.

The kitten became a cat and continued to live at the bookstore.

Customers would come in and have a fit over it. I didn't know there were that many cat lovers in the world, but there are. The cat became Joan's main draw and was even immortalized in a painting by a local artist.

One day the cat disappeared. No one knows what happened to it, but the thought was it had been kidnapped, or catnapped to be more specific. For whatever reason the cat was gone and stayed gone for months. But one autumn day the cat came back. Its little paws were rubbed raw from walking and it looked like it hadn't had a good meal in months.

Still whatever instinct there is in animals had paid off. The cat had come home. Jubilation was everywhere. People flocked to the bookstore to marvel at the return of the cat. It was the closest thing to a miracle people had seen or heard about in years.

Like I said, Joan is now living in the North. The cat has long since died, and only my memory keeps them both with me. But on a moonlit night, if you are downtown in Perry, Georgia, look in the window of the bookstore. You might just see a cat sleeping the night away. And through the mist of memory you might even catch a glimpse of Joan and me sitting before the fire talking about books.

Accident Blues

I try to be a careful driver. I really do. And since I got a new car a year ago I have tried to be a very defensive driver. I wanted that new car to be like new forever. News flash! It didn't stay that way.

As I was coming back from lunch a few weeks ago I pulled up to wait for a parking space to become vacant. An elderly man came out of the store, got into his car, and before I knew it he was backing into me. I blew the horn and hollered but he hit me anyway.

Now why didn't I throw the car in reverse or forward and get out of there, I don't know. I think I was in shock. I kept thinking he would stop but he didn't. Now what good I thought the hollering would do is the question. If he couldn't hear my horn, he certainly wouldn't hear me yelling.

The damage to my car was not bad and the gentleman was very apologetic. But I did get a little frustrated when he asked me why I hadn't blown my horn to warn him. When I responded that I had, he said he hadn't heard it. And when I asked why he didn't look before he backed up, he said he just didn't.

After we called the police, they wrote up the report exactly how we said it happened. He backed out and hit me. There was no disputing the facts.

When I asked if the "hitter" had insurance he said he did, but the card he showed me indicated it was expired. When I pointed this out to him, he said it was the wrong one. He assured me he had insurance. He also said that his wife had kept up with all this for him but she now had Alzheimer's so he had to do it all.

Anyway, I said I would just get it all from the accident report. When I went to the police station and asked for a copy they complied, but I had to pay for it. It's like five dollars and all they do is run it through a copier and hand it to you.

Then you have to deal with the insurance adjuster, make arrangements to get your car in to a body shop, and then get a rental car. It's especially trying when you live in one place and work in another.

The car came back looking better than it did before it was hit. It was shiny and repainted and even washed. People in my office said they couldn't believe how good and clean it looked.

So my advice is to drive defensively. Watch out for the other guy. And never plan for your new car to stay like new for very long. It just doesn't happen that way. Big cars will back into you before you can blink an eye—or honk a horn and holler—and then the fun really begins.

The Brother Takes a Wife

My father is a survivor. A few days ago it dawned on me that out of all his brothers and sisters, he is the only one still living. His brother T. L. died as a teenager. His brother Lewis died in early adulthood. Charlie, Russell, and Lynn were older men when they died. Lillian and Alma Ruth both lived to be in their eighties.

My father was close to his siblings. Of all his brothers, he was closest to T. L. At least, that's what he has told me. I never knew Uncle T. L. but have heard about him all my life. He was bright, good looking, and a good athlete. Everyone loved T. L., but the one who had his heart was Florence Adair. They fell in love, and even though they were both teenagers, they made plans for the future.

But one day T. L. was riding in a car with some friends and there was an accident. He was killed. Florence thought her life was over, too.

In the years that followed, Florence lived in the neighborhood where I grew up. For many years it was her and her mother, Miss Pearl, in the house up the street. Then after Miss Pearl's death, it was just Florence. When my mother became ill with cancer, Florence was a good friend to her. And after her death Florence and my father married.

The amazing thing is that almost this exact story played out in my wife Terry's family. Her father had a younger brother named Danny. He was engaged to Mary Lou Madison, but then World War II came along and turned everybody's lives upside down. Both Danny and his brother Joe went off to war.

When the war was over Joe returned, but Danny did not. He had died in battle. It was hard for the Milliard family to pick up the pieces and it was hard for Mary Lou Madison to get over her loss. But eventually she did and ended up marrying Joe Millard, my wife's father.

It's so strange how life works things out for us. Just when you think the days are at their darkest, something comes along and brightens them. Love seems blotted out by death but comes back even stronger.

I don't see history repeating itself in my case. My brother is divorced and he and Terry don't have anything in common. Even if I was out of the picture, I don't think my brother Thom would be a contender for her heart. That is one family tradition that doesn't stand a chance of repeating itself in this generation.

My Mentor, My Friend

There is another "most interesting person" in my life, and he is another one who used to live in Perry. His name is Bobby Branch, and he is the person who got me started on a writing career.

Bobby was the editor of the *Houston Home Journal* when I first moved to Perry back in the 70s. I didn't meet him right off when I came to town, but slowly got to know of him as I settled into the community.

The *Houston Home Journal (HHJ)* was recognized then as being one of the best small-town newspapers in the state and maybe the South. Bobby had the magic touch.

I wasn't brave enough to go to the office and ask to write for the paper, instead I sent in an article and waited to see if it was published. And sure enough it was. Shortly thereafter Bobby called me at home and asked if I would like to write for the *HHJ*. Since I was already employed full time at the Air Force base, I wasn't looking for a full time job, but I was interested in doing some part-time writing.

Magnanimously, Bobby offered me a column. As a matter of fact he offered me a column on anything I wanted to write about. When I hesitated he asked me what my main interest was. When I said movies he said that was what my column should be about and he would expect my first column that week.

I know those first efforts were painful for Bobby to read and even more painful to print. Still he stuck with me. He was never anything but supportive and always made comments about a particular part of the article so that I would know he had read every word I wrote. To a neophyte journalist, this was like manna from Heaven.

I wrote a weekly column for Bobby from that week until he sold the paper and moved away. I loved being on his "staff" and every year when he had his Christmas office party, I was included. I came to be friends with not only Bobby but the entire gang who worked with him. Joe, Phil, June, Emily, Terry, and others became people I not only admired but enjoyed.

Bobby had a knack for inspiring people to want to do their best. No matter how late it was on the night before the paper was printed, I could usually find four or five people working away to make sure the best and latest news was included.

After Bobby moved away, I worked for some more nice people at the *HHJ*, but they could never replace Bobby Branch. He had been my "discoverer" and the one who held my most intense loyalty. He was one of a kind.

When I started writing for Bobby, he seemed like a wise older man to me. In reality, I think we were just about the same age if he wasn't a year or two younger. I guess the reason he seemed older was because I had so much respect for him. Respect usually comes with age. I could never think of us as peers.

A few years after Bobby moved away, he was killed in a car wreck. He died much too young. At his funeral, the old crowd was reassembled, and we talked about the good times we had had.

The *Houston Home Journal* of the Bobby Branch era was a group and place that will never be replaced in my mind or heart. I've written a lot of columns since then, and I hope I have improved from where I started. Most of all, I hope Bobby is proud that he got me started.

One Book at a Time

Generally, I read at least one book a week. People seem astounded when I say this, but it is true. I usually have a book with me at all times. I read when I eat, and I read between movies. That last occurrence is when I go to the movies and get there at the wrong time, after the movie has already started. I usually just go on in and then stay until the movie starts again and I watch up to where I came in. When I am between the end of the movie and the start of the movie I move under a light and read until the film starts back.

I read anything and everything, but my favorites are usually the best-sellers. I pore over the list from *The New York Times* or *Publishers Weekly* and study which books are about to make the top ten and which ones are falling out of the race.

Movies and books are two of my favorite things along with raindrops on roses and whiskers on kittens (Sorry, I couldn't resist.). Since I enjoy movies so much, I started movie clubs in Macon and Warner Robins. They have been very successful and usually draw anywhere from thirty to forty people per session.

A month or so ago a nice lady from Barnes & Noble in Macon called me and asked if I wanted to start a movie club that would meet in their store. I explained that I already had a movie club. She then asked if maybe I would like to have it meet at their store. I answered that I didn't think they had the room. She assured me that they did but backed down quickly when I said I had thirty to forty people at each meeting.

A week or so later we talked again and this time we discussed having a book club at Barnes & Noble. We decided that meeting every week would be too much so we would limit it to once a month. And I insisted I didn't want it to be some stuffy and formal meeting. I wanted it to be fun. So "Jackie K's Best Sellers Books Club" was born. My club meets the last Tuesday in the month at Barnes & Noble from 7:00 P.M. to 8:00 P.M.

Last month, the book we all read was *Acts of Love* by Judith Michael. I actually got up the nerve to call the publisher of this book and got the name of Judith Michael's agent. I then got the number for the author(s) and called them. I say "them" because Judith Michael is actually a husband and wife writing team. The wife's name is Judith and the husband's name is Michael

I am determined to teach the world to love books like I do—one book at a time. All it takes is a little patience, a little exposure, and a loyal book club at the local bookstore.

George Washington Knew Best

A movie titled *Liar, Liar* is one of the most popular comedies in theaters this spring. It concerns an attorney whose son wishes that his father would have to tell the truth for an entire day and his wish comes true.

For many people that would be a major problem. Lying seems to have become the American way of life. "Why tell the truth when a lie would do" seems to be the new American credo. The question is why.

It seems truth tellers are more often criticized than liars. Bluntness is looked upon as a social blunder whereas a little white lie is not. There's something strange and skewed in that logic.

This trend has come to my attention in my own life lately. I know for a fact I have been involved in business dealings where the person I have been talking to has just lied flat out. And when confronted they just lied again. And they covered that lie with another lie and so on and so on.

How can they do it? Isn't there any shame in lying anymore? When I talked to a friend of mine about it, he said that is how it is in business today. If you aren't a good liar, then you aren't a good businessperson.

Now don't get me wrong, I am not 100 percent truthful. I have been known to hear the phone ring and say, "Whoever it is, tell them I am not here." Or in the past I have uttered those infamous words: "The check is in the mail."

But even when I make these little contradictions of truth, I have the decency to feel bad about it. And if I am confronted by one of my transgressions, I am embarrassed. I am not so far gone that I am a shameless liar.

I saw a survey the other day concerning which celebrities are the most trusted in America today. Jimmy Stewart led the list. Well, good for old Jimmy, except I don't think he has spoken out publicly in ten years or more. He gets his trust by default. He doesn't say anything, so people can trust what he doesn't say.

I was thinking about my friends and the ones I know that I can really, truly trust. Most would lie to keep from hurting my feelings but I have a few who would be brutally blunt if I asked them to be. Those are the people I trust the most. We really do need to get back to the feeling that a person's word is his or her bond.

As I seem to learn over and over as I grow older, the words of the wise men of the past are still true today. George Washington once said, "I cannot tell a lie." That is something we all need to emulate even 200 years after he said it.

My Mother's Rings

Since Mother's Day has come and gone, I can put down my thoughts about it. This is not the easiest day of the year for me and hasn't been since I was fourteen years old and my mother died. I suspect that for a large segment of the population this is a day that is best endured and not looked forward to with any enthusiasm.

I have always thought that the loss of my mother would get easier with each year's passing, but it hasn't. There is and has been something in my soul that aches whenever a reminder of her occurs, and what I have missed by her not being in my life. That is particularly true with my son Sean's wedding approaching. I know how excited she would be.

On the day before Mother's Day, Terry and I went to Clinton to see my father and stepmother. Daddy is about the same and so is Florence. He is much too thin and so is she, but I have to say they're both holding their own. When we took them out to lunch, they both ate well and seemed to enjoy it.

I am amazed at how wonderfully patient Florence is with Daddy. He talks about the same things over and over and she acts each time like it is something new. And when he is walking, she is right there with her hand under his elbow to keep him on balance. She is protective, supportive, and loving. He could not live without her.

We even talked some about how Daddy would come to live with me if anything (God forbid) happened to her. She seemed to need that assurance that he would be taken care of in the future.

Before we left, Florence said she had found something she wanted me to have. She went up to the front of the house and while she was gone Daddy said he didn't know what she was getting. When she returned she handed me a ring case. Inside there were two rings and I knew instantly what they were. They were my mother's rings.

Florence said she had discovered them in with some papers of Daddy's recently and wanted me to have them. I was overwhelmed. I could immediately see in my mind those rings on my mother's finger and I recalled with a great deal of emotion how they had become looser and looser as she lost her battle with cancer.

Just having something personal of my mother's was everything to me. It was like reaching across time and having her back in a small way. What I will do with the rings, I don't know. They aren't big diamonds or anything, but they are priceless in my eyes.

Celebration!

We have a wedding coming up in my family and as it approaches I know I am getting nostalgic about everything. I look at my son Sean and I see him as a little boy, not as a grown man getting ready to get married. My wife and I seem to spend a lot of time reminiscing about his early years, and every time we think back we get teary.

He is so loveable and sweet that he is easy to reminisce about. From his birth on, he has been a joy. He has been, in short, a celebration. That is a good way to describe him, and it is also the way my ex-sister-in-law always described her children. I always thought it sounded a bit dingy when she used the word, but now I know what she meant.

It also is the way I feel about my life these days. It is one celebration after another. I knew when I moved to Perry that it was the place God meant for me to be and it certainly has been. It is everything and more that anyone could want in a town, and with the wedding coming up, I have never felt so close to the place and the people.

A few weeks ago some of our friends threw a party for Sean and his fiancée Paula. It was one of those drop-in things with people coming and going for two hours. Everybody who came was truly one of my best friends.

All of the people who gave the party were my best friends, too. I wanted to freeze-frame the moments and keep them forever. I was teary to overflowing, and I wondered how I got so lucky to know such loving people.

That is the special thing about Perry. I don't think there is another place in the world that gives you the glow Perry does. I knew it the first day I came within its city limits, and I still think it now. It is a one-of-a-kind town.

Now, I know not everyone feels that way. I have had people tell me they would never want to live in Perry. It is too slow, too stuffy, too closed. Bunk! It is none of those things. At least not in the negative sense. I meet new people every day and every week and they just add to the roster of wonderful individuals in my lucky life.

Just the other day I was talking with two of my relatively new friends. We started our friendship over our love for books and it has grown from there. As I sat in their den talking with them, the subject turned to fans. I confessed that I run an electric fan 365 days a year. Amazingly, they said they did the same thing, and their children do, too.

Now where else could you find people with whom you have so much in common. Books, fans, children, and a million other things draw me to the town I have learned to love so much. My family is a celebration; my town is a celebration; my life is a celebration!

Let's Hear it for the Mouse

A few weeks ago I went to New York because Disney was having a gala celebration for the movie *Hercules* and they had invited me. I had asked that I be able to do newspaper and TV interviews but the answer came back that there was only room for me to do print.

Because I was only doing print interviews, I was scheduled to see the movie Wednesday night and do the interviews on Thursday morning. This left me free to fly back to Georgia on Thursday night. This really suited me better since that Friday was my anniversary and also some of our friends were giving a barbecue for Sean and Paula (the engaged couple) on Friday night.

Now anyone who has known me for any length of time knows how I hate to fly, so the idea of me blithely hopping on a plane to fly to New York on one day and then coming back the next is a little ludicrous. But I did want those interviews.

The flight up was not bad. Delta was ready when I was, and the weather was clear. The only flaw was those stupid little bag lunches they now offer. You pick them up as you board the plane and they are most miserly.

When I arrived at my hotel, the person checking me in said, "Ah, Mr. Cooper, you will be with us for two nights." And I said, "Ah no, I will be here for one night only." But they insisted Disney had me booked for two nights. The mouse has money, so I figured it was no big deal.

When I got to the Disney hospitality suite the lady who handles TV interviews for Disney called me over to tell me she had to change some of my interviews on Friday. When I told her I wasn't doing TV and that I wouldn't be there on Friday she said, "Sure you are." When I mentioned that I had a plane ticket back on Thursday, she told me not to worry about it, for it would be changed. The mouse has connections.

The hotel where I was staying looked over Central Park and it was a beautiful view. Summer in New York fills the streets with people riding bikes, roller-blading, and doing all the New York things. Watching all that exercise made me hungry, so I ordered room service. I asked for a hamburger, fries, extra tomatoes, and pickles, extra ice, and two diet cokes. It took less than an hour to get there and the bill was only forty-one dollars. All together now: "The mouse has money!"

Later that night we were all bused to a screening of *Hercules*. It was such a big theater you had to go up two flights of escalators to get to the screen. Once I had finished watching it, I decided the music in the movie was good, but the music in *Beauty and the Beast* was better. That is how I judge these animated movies from Disney. Their value depends on how good their songs are.

The next morning I took the van out to the pier where the *Hercules* interviews were being held. I didn't have a jacket and I didn't have a sweater. I did have a hearty appetite and was looking forward to the breakfast buffet they had promised. Being a Southern man, I was anticipating eggs, and bacon, toast, and grits. What I got was bagels and more bagels.

With so little to eat, I was freezing. I had planned to stoke my internal fires with food, but a bite of bagel will not keep you warm. So I shivered and chattered until a mouse person provided me with an official *Hercules* sweater.

I wore it when I talked with Tate Donovan (the voice of Hercules). Warmly, I even asked him about Jennifer Aniston, his new squeeze and the woman who plays Rachel on *Friends*. He said they were fine and she was fine and her show was fine and her new movie was fine.

I wore it when I talked with Alan Menken, the composer of all the good mouse music. He has won eight Oscars, and I told him he should just melt them down into one Big Oscar. He thought that was very clever.

I wore it when I talked with Michael Bolton and heard him say he might cut his hair because he wants to be a movie actor. My advice was hold on to the hair until you actually get a role in a movie. Stick with the singing and pray the song "Go the Distance" (from *Hercules*) has the mouse good fortune to be an Oscar winner. Bolton needs a hit. He knows it and I know it and the mouse knows it.

When all the interviews were over, I got ready to get on the van and go back to the hotel. I still had to go out and buy a shirt and tie for the TV interviews the next day. Just as I got ready to step into the van, this mouse person I didn't know said the mouse wanted the sweater back. I couldn't believe it. It was a great sweater—a pullover. And now they wanted it back. They literally took it from me, pulling it over my head and messing up my strands of hair.

When I got back to the hotel I ordered another forty-dollar hamburger and then set out to find a shirt and tie.

As I turned the corner from my hotel, The Gap was waiting. Walking in like I shopped at The Gap every day. I picked out a blue shirt and tie and flipped the credit card to the "oh, so charming" salesperson. "A wonderful selection," she told me and she was right. Me, the mouse, and The Gap were on a roll.

On my second and final night in New York for the press junket for *Hercules*, the rest of the TV critics went to see the movie. I had been told to be out back of the Essex Hotel and someone would take me to Gabriel's, where the mouse was throwing a dinner party.

Ever punctual, I was on the spot where I was supposed to be at 8:15 P.M. sharp. A bus—yes, a big fifty-seat bus—pulled up and the driver said he was looking for the people from Disney. When I told him I was the only person from Disney going to Gabriel's the driver looked much impressed. So was I—it isn't every day you travel on a bus by yourself.

The meal was a complete success since I ate with people from *E! Entertainment*. And the next day these same people introduced me to Art Mann. Everyone else was going crazy and shouting, "There's Joel Siegel." Me, I was shaking hands with Art the Man.

When we arrived the next day to do the interviews, we were all sent to the makeup room. Well, at least some of us were. The lady applying the goo to my face told me all about her singing lessons in between choruses of "A Whole New World." I think she thought the mouse was listening.

But she did make a comment about my eyes. "Such pretty blue eyes," she said. "And you wore a blue shirt to make them look bluer." Then she broke the spell by adding, "These eyes look mighty tired, though." Splat! The ego had landed.

I did get through the interview and then had a non-English-speaking taxi driver take me to the airport. I said things like "We have to go pronto!" "Speedy!" "Step on it!"

I staggered into the airport, where it seems all the flights out of LaGuardia had been delayed because of bad weather. My 3:00 P.M. flight to Atlanta had been canceled; the 4:00 P.M. was temporarily delayed; and the 5:00 P.M. was scheduled to leave at 6:30 P.M.

A siege mentality developed among those of us who were waiting for a plane—any plane. I met a mother and daughter who just had to get back to Atlanta, so her daughter could start modeling and actress classes. This little girl was six years old and immediately broke into her version of "Tomorrow" from "Annie." I guess she thought I was a talent scout.

My flight finally boarded at 7:30 P.M. and we sat on the runway for another hour because of thunderstorms. I got home after midnight on the night of my son's party and my anniversary. I had an excuse the mouse had written but the Disney charm only goes so far.

God Knows

This year has flown by. It was just yesterday that my son Sean and his girlfriend Paula got engaged. It was supposed to be a *loooooooong* engagement and already it is here. There is only one more day till their vows are said.

Yes, theirs is one more wedding to attend. I have only been to a hundred this summer, but this is the *big* one. Sean has said that he wants everyone who attends to be glad they did. He wants nothing somber, nothing too formal.

I want the world to be there to share it with me, but unfortunately I couldn't invite the world. I could only invite a small group of friends and relatives, and that means I left some people out who probably wonder where their invitations are.

Those who know me know that I am a person who likes to please people. I hate to think that anyone might be offended by being invited (Who is Sean Cooper?) or not invited (We've known Jackie Cooper forever). So if I did do the wrong thing in any way, it was inadvertent. I honestly had the best of intentions.

Now let me switch to a positive mode. This whole year of planning has been a wonderful experience. I knew I had great friends, but I was wrong: I have the most exceptionally wonderful friends in the world. From the parties to the rehearsal dinner to those who have told me that they usually don't go to weddings but will be there for this one, it has been a great experience.

And then there is one special person I want to mention. Her name is Margaret. She's been supportive of my writing for some time now. Unfortunately, a month or so ago she told me she wouldn't be seeing me for a while because she was sick and was going to have to have treatments for her illness.

A few days ago a friend of mine told me she had been to see Margaret in order to do a few things for her. While she was there, Margaret asked my friend if she would do her a favor. She said, "You know Jackie Cooper, don't you?"

My friend said she did and Margaret replied, "Well, I read everything he writes, and I just love Jackie Cooper. You know his boy is getting married, and I have made him some pillowcases. Would you make sure he gets them?"

Honestly, it just doesn't get any better than this. With all her troubles and things on her mind, she thought about my Sean. Plus she said she loved me, and I love her too. I have told all of my friends to keep Margaret in their prayers. All they have to do is pray for Jackie Cooper's friend. God knows who she is.

My Son's Wedding Weekend

It happened. Yes, the wedding really did take place, as did the rehearsal and the rehearsal supper. It all has been done and is over. Now all that is left is the shouting, or maybe I should say the crying. That, I think, will continue for some time.

The day of the rehearsal/rehearsal dinner was a tense one. I was in a snappy mood and that doesn't make for good relations. Just try, however, driving two-and-a-half hours to meet your parents, and then turn around and drive two-and-a-half hours back. J. J., my older son and the *single* one, and I drove up in his car and met my folks in Washington GA.

On the way up, I got basic driving instructions from J. J. Sure, it was his car, *but* I do know how to drive. Still, it was constant: "Don't go so fast." "Don't tailgate." "Don't pass like that." "Don't stay in that gear." It's not like I haven't been driving for a hundred years. He wanted me to drive his way.

When we got the folks back to Perry, the other relatives began to arrive. Well, most of them did. Terry's younger brother left a message on our answering machine saying his car had broken down. Then we got a second call from him saying he wasn't going to be able to make it.

When we got to the church for the rehearsal, J. J. and the group from the motel arrived late. I had sent him out to guide them to the rehearsal. His excuse for being late? Uncle Alan and Cousin Brie had gotten stuck in an elevator. Now there is not a building in Perry, Georgia, that requires an elevator but they had gotten stuck in one.

The rehearsal dinner had been planned for outside but Hurricane Danny had made rain a real possibility. As a matter of fact, the sky had opened up that afternoon. I asked my wife Terry what we would do if it rained. Her answer was—she didn't know. Have you ever prayed "Please, please, please, please don't rain" and meant it? I did. Over and over again. And it didn't rain.

The rehearsal dinner was like something out of *House Beautiful*. Friends of ours had turned their magnificent house over to us and we had tables set up around their pool. The temperature was fine since the rain had cooled things off and the food was delicious.

I managed to make a toast to the happy couple that thanked all of our guests for coming. I kept asking Terry if I was leaving anyone out. She said no, but later I realized I had left out my son's new in-laws. That is really not good for future relationships.

The next day the wedding went off without a hitch. As the married couple turned to leave the altar the pianist charged into "Oh Happy Day!" It was the perfect touch to a celebration of joy. And it almost had them dancing in the aisles. At a Baptist church yet!

Do As I Say, Not As I Did

Is there a secret to being the parent of adult children? I need an answer quickly. I think I did pretty well being a parent as long as my kids were under my roof and under my direction, but now that they are grown it is a difficult thing not to open your mouth and give an opinion—an opinion you expect to be followed.

For instance, my married son Sean called to let me know he was buying a computer. My first reaction was to scream, "Have you lost your mind?" But I didn't do that. Instead I asked him about cost, terms, etc. He was so excited about getting it that he was foaming at the mouth. I was also foaming but for a different reason. Still I held my tongue and just said great, great, great.

Having gotten through that test, I moved to test number 2 (God is giving me these tests to see how well I do.). The newlyweds came home last week. They arrived on Wednesday and were staying until Sunday. I asked what time they were leaving on Sunday. The answer was seven or eight that night. When I pointed out that would put them getting into Kentucky around four in the morning, my son smiled and said, "We will split the driving." When I pointed out that Paula had to be a work at seven in the morning on Monday, he answered she could sleep in the car while he drove.

Again, I smiled and kept my mouth shut. But when Sunday came they left at four in the afternoon. They had changed their minds about the right time to leave. Of course, they still didn't get to Kentucky until midnight, and I was awake all night waiting for a call telling me their car had broken down.

Still, I reminded my wife that these two incidents sounded like something from when we were first married. One time, we were going to Florida to visit my in-laws, and I decided it was dumb to wait until morning to leave for the drive down. It was midnight and I was wide awake, so we hopped in the car and started out. We had gone less than a hundred miles when I began to feel like I had to have some sleep. We had to stop virtually at every rest stop between Valdosta, Georgia, and St Petersburg, Florida, for me to grab a few winks of sleep. When we finally got to Terry's parents' home the next morning, they were aghast we had driven all night. I couldn't understand why they were upset.

Another time, we called both sets of parents and told them we were moving to California. You could have heard the wails out on the West Coast. After their sobs had subsided to whimpers, I told them we planned to drive both our cars across country. I didn't want to mess with towing a vehicle. Oh yes, and we planned to communicate by walkie-talkies.

I thought Terry's father was going to have a stroke. He sputtered and fumed for hours, but my mind was made up. It was my family, my cars, and my trip. In two cars, we would go. Now I understand how stupid that whole thing sounded and how foolish it was to take my family on that kind of cross-country excursion, but I didn't see it that way then.

It seems the perspectives of youth and older age are not the same. But, hopefully, I can remember myself at the ages of my sons and understand how they feel. It's either that or buy a muzzle for my wife and me.

Being Committed

My youngest son Sean got married a few weeks ago. When I watched him and his bride standing at the altar, I was struck by the vows of commitment they made. What they pledged really spelled out how they are supposed to be committed to each other now and forever.

Commitment is, or should be, a big thing in our lives. We need commitment to our spouse, our kids, our parents, our church, and our jobs. I have to say this is a lesson my parents instilled in me at an early age. If I started something, I was expected to finish it. Therefore, there were no teams I could quit, no subjects I could drop. Believe me, being the non-athlete that I am, there were many, many times I wanted to quit something I had foolishly joined.

My parents also believed in a strong work ethic. That meant at age thirteen I was expected to work on the weekends. Even during the school year, I worked.

My employer was Johnson Brothers Supermarket, and I was the bag boy and shelf stocker. I earned the grand fee of fifty cents an hour, which meant my total paycheck on Saturday night was six dollars. The problem was that I ate about eight dollars worth of junk while I worked. I always ended up owing my employers' money on Saturday night, or at least my father did. He would have to bail me out when he picked me up.

Even operating at a loss, I was still expected to work. I worked for the Johnson Brothers until I started college. Then in college, I worked as a waiter in the dining hall. In the summers, I was everything from a camp counselor to a roadman for the highway department.

After college I went into the military. No Canada for me. Vietnam was raging, but I was still expected to serve. Luckily I spent my entire four-year tour of duty in the Air Force at Robins Air Force Base.

When that commitment was completed, I headed to Rocky Mount, North Carolina, to work for Hardee's Food Systems. I had only worked for them a year when I was offered a job with the legal office at Robins. I remember clearly how my friend Louis Rickman in Rocky Mount, advised me not to take the job. He cautioned that if I started jumping from one job to another I would be doing it the rest of my life. Well, I made only one jump and I have been a government employee ever since.

The point is that I never, ever quit one job before I had another one lined up. I see people quit in a huff and stay unemployed for months while they find something new. I just couldn't do that. I have to have security. I have to have commitment.

Yes, Sean and Paula are going to learn what commitment is all about in the next few years. There will be jobs they will be tempted to quit, and, even their marriage will have its down side from time to time. All marriages do. But a committed relationship is the best kind of all.

Being committed to what we do is a trait we all need to pass along to our children and one we need to practice ourselves.

Soul Mates

Certain couples exude happiness. They seem to be so happy just being in the presence of each other that you feel warm and fuzzy just sharing their affection. These people I call "soul mates," and I believe they are people who are fated to be together.

Now, sometimes we don't find our soul mate. In those instances, we make do with what we find. But if we are really lucky we find that special someone who completes us. My friends Marvin and Linda met these criteria.

Linda was the first person in the couple I met. She and I judged the Miss Senior Warner Robins Contest together. As soon as we met I knew I had found someone whose company I would enjoy. We were "soul friends" from the start.

After that meeting, Linda joined my movie club and soon her husband, Marvin, followed. In time, their daughter and her husband would become members. They all loved the movies, and I, in turn, loved all of them. In a sense, they completed me.

Eighteen months ago, Marvin had some health problems and died soon thereafter. Linda and her family were devastated. I grieved with them because I had lost a friend, and I worried about Linda because she was so lost without Marvin. Also, she had had some health problems that were aggravated by her grief.

Still, she was a trooper. She came to the movie club in a wheelchair and later, as she grew stronger, walking with a cane. Every time she came she had a big smile on her face. I never saw her cry. I never heard her complain. If I hadn't been hearing from her daughter about how rough things were for her, I would have thought she was doing just great.

I loved having her in the movie club because when I would say something she found funny, I would hear that deep chuckle of hers. It wasn't a laugh per se but a deep rich sound of enjoyment that was distinctly Linda.

A few weeks ago, she came by my office to see me. She looked fabulous. A redhead, she always seemed to brighten the world around her—even when she was standing outside in the full sun. On this day, she was walking with a cane but had that big smile blazing. I commented on how great she looked, and she said she thought life was getting better.

We talked for only a short time since she had her grandson with her. I gave her a hug, told her how great she was, and walked her to her car. That was the last time I saw her. A few nights ago, her daughter called me and said Linda had died of a heart attack. I could believe just as easily that it was of a broken heart.

"Soul mates" have a hard time keeping it together when their partner leaves. I don't think the world was ever the same for Linda after Marvin's death. But I am a believer in souls, and I believe they are together now.

The world has lost some of its glow with them gone, and I can't help but miss them. Still, their "soul friend" knows Linda's broken heart has been mended. They are now part of eternity and partners for eternity.

Return to Niagara Falls

It had been ten years since I visited the Niagara Falls area, but the city and the falls still looked the same when I paid a recent visit. I had to be in the city of Niagara Falls last week on business and finally convinced myself, on the fourth day of my visit, that the falls were worth seeing again.

One reason I hesitated was that I wanted to eat at the restaurant perched on top of one of those "sky needles," and it's on the Canadian side. That means you have to go through that mess of passing across the border. Now I don't do drugs, so I know I am clean. But there is always that thought in your head about the unknown stranger who might have sneaked something into your car.

There was a crowd of us that went over. One was a lady from the area and since I was driving, she gave me instructions on how to handle the border guards. "When they ask where you are from say the United States," she told me gravely, "don't say Georgia. They don't like smart alecks, so answer United States to everything. Don't do anything to make them think you are acting smart."

The first question the border guard asked me was indeed as she had predicted.

Easy. I answered, "the United States."

Then he asked where was I born.

Again I said, "the United States."

"Where?" he asked, looking hostile.

"The United States," I answered.

He then stood up and came over to the car.

"Where in the United States?" he asked.

"Georgia," I replied meekly. And with that he passed us through the gate. I was already dreading the return inquisition.

Sure enough when we were on the way back I got questioned again. I was asked what I had been doing in Canada. "Nothing," I replied. Wrong answer, folks.

"Nothing?" he asked.

"Well, just eating," I answered, beginning to sweat.

"Whose car is this?" he said, changing tactics.

"A rental," I said quickly, as he looked at the innocent white car with a gleam in his eyes.

"Okay, on your way," he muttered. He didn't say anything else but he still looked suspicious.

As I sped across the bridge and back to the land of the free, I expected guards to jump out at any time and shoot my tires. Thankfully, they didn't.

While we were at the restaurant, I was surprised to learn that people still talk about the old Marilyn Monroe movie *Niagara* whenever they see the falls. There were Marilyn posters in many of the shops, and people were constantly pointing out to me where such and such scene from the movie had been shot.

"She met her boyfriend there," they said referring to the meeting in the movie.

"She got killed over there," they added.

Now that I am back home, I have got to rent the film just so I can put all that knowledge to use. I want to compare how these places looked in reality and how they looked on film.

In the world of reality, the restaurant was great, even if it was twelve stories up in the air. To get there, you have to ride one of these outside elevators that was created just to make me miserable. But, once up top, I was okay, and I did like the way it revolved to show off the falls.

As night came, the lights were turned on around the falls, and you could hear everyone oohing and aahing. It was a magical sight. I can understand why people still flock to see this wonder of the world year after year.

So did I have a good time? I sure did. But I still have that deep down feeling that every place I want to go and every place I want to see are located within the original forty-eight states—the ones where you don't have to fly to get there, and you don't have to cross any foreign borders.

BIG DIEHL

One of the most exciting aspects of my writing career has been the opportunity to interview celebrities. I've had a chance to meet and interview such stars as Julia Roberts, Mel Gibson, Oprah Winfrey, and John Travolta. Although I would like to say I am their new best friend, in truth, I can only say I have met with them briefly. But that is not the case with author William Diehl. Him I do consider a friend.

Bill is the author of such notable books as *Sharkey's Machine*, *Primal Fear*, and *Show of Evil*. I met him several years ago when I was asked to profile him for *Georgia Journal Magazine*.

He lives at St. Simon's Island so I made the trip down and spent an afternoon with him. He was the perfect host and the perfect interview subject. We talked for hours, and I felt as if I really got to know him.

Bill is married to Virginia Gunn, who was the weather person for the ABC affiliate in Atlanta. She has retired from TV and now is involved in local politics. While meeting Bill, I also had the chance to meet her. I was doubly impressed that day.

In the course of the day, Bill not only gave me a great interview, he also autographed copies of his books for me. I always appreciate when an author does this, and I keep these copies on a special section of my bookcase at home.

Just about every time Bill comes out with a new book, I talk with him. Sometimes it is in person, and sometimes it is by phone. He always gives me some great insight about his characters and some reason for a plot twist.

I knew when I read *Primal Fear* it was a big Diehl. This courtroom drama was the most insightful dramatic story Bill had tackled, and readers ate it up. After the book was made into a movie, starring Richard Gere, even more readers were drawn to it. The lead character, attorney Martin Vail, and his nemesis, Aaron Stampler, came back for another battle in the sequel, *Show of Evil*.

A few months ago I was at home paying bills, when the phone rang. As I answered it, a gravelly voice said, "Diehl here!" Yep, it was my buddy Bill, telling me he had a new novel being released in November and saying he wanted me to read it. It was the third and final installment of the *Primal Fear* trilogy, and it was titled *Reign in Hell*. Once again Martin Vail and Aaron Stampler do battle, and this time to the death.

A few days later, I received an autographed copy of the galleys for the book. I devoured the story in only a few sittings. After I finished the book, I called Bill to let him know how much I enjoyed it. During our conversation, he mentioned he was going on an author's tour in October. I told him I wished he could come by my area and sign some copies. Bill, being Bill, immediately gave me the name of his representative at Ballantine Books.

I passed this information on to a friend of mine who works for Barnes and Nobles Booksellers in Macon, and, in the flash of an eye, Bill was scheduled for a book signing at the store. Even better, he agreed to speak to my book club while in town.

Bill did come to Macon and he did appear at my book club. He was warm, witty, and incredibly intelligent. People lined up to speak to him and get some books autographed. Best of all, over and over he referred to me as his friend Jackie Cooper.

Julia doesn't call, Mel and I haven't spoken in years, Oprah is just too busy to stay in touch, and John is off somewhere flying his plane; but my buddy Bill still e-mails or calls ever so often. I know, too, that when his next book is finished he will send it to me to get my opinion.

William Diehl is a big deal in the world of authors and in my small world he is a close personal friend.

Good Grief

My wife and I made a trip to Wilmore, Kentucky, recently. This was the second time we had visited this special little town. The first was the week before my son Sean's wedding and we had carried up things for the newlyweds' apartment. On that occasion, my wife had cried for the entire eight hours of the trip back to Perry.

This time when we went it was to visit the three-month-married couple. Boy, what a strange feeling that is. We broke the trip in Cleveland, Tennessee, and went on to Wilmore the next morning. When we got started on this second leg of our trip, it was foggy and overcast. I had an idea the entire weekend was going to be that way. The clouds stayed with us all the way until we got outside Lexington, Kentucky. Just as we came up a hill, the clouds disappeared and the sun was shining. It was beautiful weather in beautiful country.

We got to Sean and Paula's in time for lunch. Since my wife does not eat beef, Paula had fixed chicken and rice for us. They had purchased Diet Coke and even bought me a tomato. In the cupboard were some cheese tidbits which are also my favorite. Knowing they had done this just to be prepared for us was so touching. However, they had not bought me a can of tomato juice as their budget would stand only so much.

That afternoon we went shopping and then to a movie. I always have to see a movie and this time the only thing I hadn't

seen was a thriller called *Most Wanted*. Sean, Paula, and my
wife were good sports and sat through it like troopers. After we
finished the film, we ate supper and then went home and
watched TV.

Since their apartment is small we had decided to stay in a
motel. When we got to our room we were surprised to find
that it was handicap-friendly. It was the only room left. It
looked like it had been designed to make everything in reach of
a person in a wheelchair. The bathroom did not have a door on
it; the closet hanger bar was very low; and the bed was close to
the floor. The next morning when I flung my feet over the side
of the bed to arise, I almost knocked my teeth out.

We went to church with the kids and then went out for
lunch. As soon as we got back to the apartment we left for our
trip home. No need to draw out the goodbyes. As the car made
its way back south, I felt some tinges of grief, but it was good
grief. I was already beginning to miss them but knowing how
happy and in love they are made it a good kind of sorrow.

Whenever I read *Peanuts* and Charlie Brown's cry of
"Good Grief!," I have wondered if this were not a contra-
diction in terms. But it isn't. Some grief is good, particularly
the kind you feel when your children grow up to be adults and
they find the right person to marry and are happy.

It took us eight hours to get back to Perry, and I was dead
tired when we arrived. Still, it was a good trip. There were no
tears this time, rather we just talked about how quickly we had
become our parents and were going to see our married
children. It was only yesterday when our folks were coming to
visit us as newlyweds. Hopefully they felt the joy and sorrow of
good grief, too.

A Potential Juror

Recently I got the chance to serve as a juror for a trial. Yes, the old summons came through the mail and found me. Being the good citizen I am, I went to court with a smile on my face and a song in my heart. (I also had a newspaper and book in my hands to carry me through the interminable days ahead if I got selected.)

As luck would have it, I didn't get chosen. (Darn that luck!) So after one very long day, I was free to go and live my life and leave the weighing of justice to others. Still, I have to admit the day of jury selection had provided me with some observations.

First of all, there was an attorney there who was especially eloquent. He spoke with intelligence and conviction about who the ideal juror would be. He explained all the questions he asked of the potential jurors and held direct eye contact up and down the line. He was impressive.

But, his tie was askew. It had somehow been turned from the center of his collar to the side of his collar. As he talked I could barely hear what he was saying for staring at this errant tie. When he had finished and we were taking a break, I walked up and straightened his tie for him. He looked at me like I had lost my mind. I looked at him like he could have lost his case. The law doesn't need distractions and this wandering tie was one of the worst.

Second, no one knows how honest he or she should be when being asked questions as a potential juror. For example, the lawyers asked if we knew the plaintiff, defendant, opposing lawyers, or any of the potential witnesses. Haven't they ever heard of "six degrees of Kevin Bacon"? All of us know somebody who knows somebody who knows somebody who ultimately leads us to the person in question. Houston County just isn't that big.

Then, there are the questions about have you ever had a broken bone? Does that include fingers, toes, nose or what? Come on, I need something more specific than that one all-encompassing question. And does a bad sprain count, too? I couldn't figure out whether or not to raise my hand or let it pass.

I was also confused about how to respond when asked if we knew anyone else on the panel of jurors. I have lived in Houston County for twenty years. I know, or know of, just about everybody. Or know somebody who knows somebody who knows just about everybody. In the court that day, I knew just about all the lawyers. I definitely knew the judge. And I could have named the clerk of the court and the court administrator as friends. What was I doing there!

Finally, there was a really unique observation. Just when you think you have heard all the possible questions attorneys ask of jurors, they spring a new one on you. At this court on this day, a lawyer asked the potential jurors whether they had bumper stickers on their cars.

One lady raised her hand. She said she had a "clergy" sticker on her car. But get this: the bumper sticker wasn't hers. It came with the car when she bought it. She said she kept it on her car since it caused people not to be hostile to her.

The attorney who had asked the question topped her response. He said when he bought his car it had a sticker on it that said, "My child is an Honor Student." He said he kept that one on his car, too.

I don't know what he wanted to know about the bumper stickers. I am sure there was some method to his madness. Maybe he wanted to know if we were the types who made political statements with our stickers. But none of us bit and he finally moved on.

Eventually, they made their choices and I was dismissed. As happy as I was to be let out, inside I was a little hurt they hadn't chosen me. It brought back all those times on the playground in grammar school when I was one of the last ones chosen for a team. I guess inside every grown man a child remains, and the child always wants to say, "Choose me! Choose me!"

Jodi Benson

In my role as an entertainment reporter, I had the chance last week to go to Atlanta and speak with Jodi Benson. Now you may not recognize the name, but she is the voice of Ariel in the Disney animated movie *The Little Mermaid*. Eight years after its original release, the film has been re-released to movie theaters, and she is on the press circuit talking about her participation in the film.

When you meet Jodi, you wonder why she hasn't made any actual screen appearances. She is as pretty as any other successful actress of today, and she exudes wholesomeness and charm. After *The Little Mermaid*'s first release, people had a chance to see her in the play *Crazy For You*. It ran on Broadway for three and a half years and she was the star. But on the screen her participation has been strictly as a voice for an animated character.

When the movie *Flubber* with Robin Williams comes out, you will hear her as the voice of his computer. She is also providing the voice of Lady in the *Lady and the Tramp* sequel that will go direct to video. She is staying busy, though most of her work is with Disney.

I told her that we are having a "Same Time Next Year" type of friendship. I interviewed her when *The Little Mermaid* was first released; then two years later she was doing a guest appearance at Disney World when I was there and I got to talk with her again. Two years after that, she was in New Orleans for the premiere of *The Hunchback of Notre Dame*. They had all the famous voice talent there for a musical extravaganza, which was filmed for the Disney Channel. We got to catch up on each other there, too.

Now, two more years later, she is in Atlanta and we pick up our conversation. I asked about her husband, Ray, who is an actor, and where they are living now. She said they had just bought a house in California and were going to see what life out there was like. When I mentioned that she should be able to get a lot of sitcom work, she answered that she would really like to do just Disney products.

This statement led to a discussion about her religious beliefs. Jodi is a devout Christian and lives her faith. She said that although she did not want to be "holier than thou," there were just certain roles she could not take because of the profanity or nudity that was required. She said she had a good agent who knew what her parameters were, and that he didn't even refer the things to her that would not be acceptable.

It was strange hearing a Hollywood person talking this way, but Jodi insists there are many more like her living in the celebrity world. One person she spoke of with much respect is Martha Williams, the force behind *Touched by an Angel* and *Promised Land*. She said Williams had done a lot to influence the television community.

When we were ending our interview, she looked at me and asked, "You're a believer, aren't you?" When I responded that I was, she said, "I thought so."

In the past, I have been asked if I was a Christian, but never if I was a believer. Somehow, that terminology made it an even warmer request for information. And it made Jodi

Benson an even more special person in my eyes. Aren't you glad that Ariel, the little mermaid, is such a fine role model for your children?

I know at times the entertainment world seems like a godless society but there are more people in show business like Jodi Benson than you would imagine. Most of them live their faith but don't discuss it publicly. For them it is a private matter.

I respect those who act that way. Still, every once in a while it is nice to meet someone who goes to Sunday School and Church like I do, and they also happen to be a celebrity. It may sound silly, but somehow it renews my faith in the goodness of humankind.

The Best Thanksgiving Ever

Lately, I have caught myself whistling "Oh, There's No Place Like Home for the Holidays." That song has such a great sentiment to it and I know that it is being heard all the way up in Kentucky. The last thing Sean said to me as he and Paula were getting into the car for the drive back to their apartment in Wilmore, Kentucky, after visiting for Thanksgiving was, "Just think, Dad: only three more weeks and we will be back."

Having kids who live away from home in another state has given me a new perspective on the holidays. As my oldest son J. J. said, "It used to be called 'Thanksgiving' but now it is 'the time when Sean and Paula will be here'"

And what a great holiday it was. They had told us they were coming in on Thanksgiving Eve but would be going straight to Hawkinsville to stay with Paula's parents, Barbara and Mike. Still, I told Sean to call me when they arrived so I would know they had gotten here safely. Well, I stayed awake until 4:00 A.M. and he still hadn't called. Terry had long since gone to sleep with the rationale that if anything was wrong Mike and Barbara would call. Okay, I knew that. Still I just wanted to hear his voice saying he was here.

The next day he told me they had gotten in after a time he considered appropriate to call. I told him there wasn't a time that was too late—not when he had said he would call! Okay, I know that is extreme, but I don't rest easy until I know they are off the road.

When they got ready to leave on Sunday, I told him to call me when they got back to Kentucky regardless of the time. That night I went to bed with the portable phone resting on my stomach. And at 12:45 A.M. it rang. They were back and they were safe, even though traffic had been terrible and it had rained on them most of the way.

Thanksgiving itself was one of our best ever. Even though we had to share them with Paula's parents, we still had them with us on Thanksgiving night. J. J. was home and we celebrated with gusto. I don't think I have ever felt so thankful for the good things in my life. And Paula, well, it was like I had always had a daughter-in-law. She was just one of us, now and forever.

My folks didn't get to come down for Thanksgiving, but they will be here for Christmas. When we called them on Thanksgiving night, we passed the phone around so everyone could speak. Before we hung up, Daddy got a little teary and I thought to myself, *Please don't start crying*. He does that. Waits until we are just about ready to hang up, or if we are visiting, just about ready to get into the car. Then he gets upset.

A few days after Thanksgiving when Sean and Paula were getting into the car and were saying goodbye I felt this flood of emotion coming over me. As soon as they pulled out of the driveway, I turned to my wife and said, "I will never, ever tell Daddy not to cry when we leave."

That old saying about how you can never know exactly how someone feels until you go through the same thing is oh, so true. Yesterday, I was the leaver. Now I am the leavee, and boy, is that a kick in the teeth.

A Special Christmas

Can you name the best Christmas you ever had? Come on, there has to be one that stands out more than others. For me, well, I have a problem deciding, too. It would have to be one since I got married, because all the ones up to that one were only so-so.

When I was a small child, my Christmases were always disappointments because I wanted a surprise; but I didn't know what it was. Therefore, I never got it and was always disappointed. Then when I reached my teen years, my mother had died, so Christmas just wasn't the same. It was just a ritual we went through, but none of us had our hearts in it.

But then I got married and I had someone to share the seasons with, and share the excitement. In truth, Terry is a much better Christmas person than I am. She really gets into Christmas from the decorating to the present giving. Me, well, I still have to be dragged into Christmas...but this year might just be different.

This year will be the first celebration with the newlyweds. Plus, my folks are coming for a few days and it will be good to have them here. Last year they didn't come and my stepmother told me they would never do that again. She said it was just not Christmas being away from family. And I feel the same way. We all need to be with people we love and cherish.

My father doesn't get too excited about many things these days, but he is excited about Christmas. That seems to penetrate the sadness that sometimes surrounds him and brightens him up the way he used to be. Having Sean and Paula home will be a special treat for him, as he has always had a special place in his heart for Sean. They can talk sports, which is something he certainly cannot do with me.

We also have set aside some time to be with our very best friends. In our lifetime in Perry, our friends have been our family. My boys did not know their real aunts and uncles that well due to distance, so the friends we had became their relatives. They were there for birthdays, holidays, and other special times. They made my boys' lives richer, and I love them all for being there and caring.

Music also influences my holiday spirit. This year, I am singing in the church cantata, which I haven't done for a while, and that makes me feel more Christmasy. The sound of the choir, the talent of the orchestra, and the decorations of the church all bring home the special spirit of Christmas. Plus, I attended a concert by the Air Force Reserve Band and it was the best I had ever heard. The soloists excelled and the band itself was in tiptop form.

One other special music treat was a CD I discovered. It's called *A Magical Christmas/Vail, Colorado* and features Kelly Jerles among the performers. Her husband, produced the Christmas CD and it is wonderful. I could listen to Kelly sing "Three Blind Mice" and be happy; so to hear her sing "Have Yourself a Merry Little Christmas" is awe-inspiring. She also sings "A Colorado Christmas," which she wrote herself. It could become a Christmas classic.

So as I anticipate the arrival of my children—home for the holidays—I think maybe this will be my best Christmas ever. But I also think about the future Christmases when there may be grandchildren anticipating Santa. Then I think that maybe my best Christmases are yet to come.

Chapter 3

Reflections from Route 98

My Life Is a 10

Another year has flown by. 1997 is gone and 1998 is here. That old adage about time going faster as you get older is true! I had just gotten used to writing 1997 on my checks and here it is 1998 already.

But what a year 1997 was. My son graduated from college, got married, and moved to Kentucky. And it all happened about that fast. Then, too, just about everyone I know had a child get married this summer. Every weekend for a month or more we went to a wedding.

As I look back at 1997, I consider it to have been a pretty good year. In addition to the wedding, my family maintained its health. My father didn't get any better, but he doesn't seem to be any worse either. I still have a family I adore, friends who make me happy, and a job that provides me with satisfaction. And as an added plus, I have all my extra things like the reviews I write, my book and movie clubs, and my stint on TV.

When I was just a little boy, my mother told me I was special. I guess all parents tell their children this, but in my case I swallowed it hook, line, and sinker. And I have had a special life. Sure, there have been some tragedies, but overall it has been one that I wouldn't swap with anyone. Who else can look back at twenty-seven years of marriage and still get chills by looking at his wife? Who else can see their children and tear up just thinking how special they are? Who else has friends who provide him with as much fun and pleasure as mine do?

And who gets to go to Hollywood and New York and interview celebrities? I think that is the most outrageous part of my life. Last year, I talked with a variety of people from the voice of Hercules (Tate Donovan) to the voice of the Little Mermaid (Jodi Benson). I saw 154 movies and a dozen or more plays. I had the chance to renew my friendship with author Bill Diehl and introduce him to my friends in the book club.

People ask me how I ever got up the nerve to do it all, and I say I just stumbled into it. That is the truth. There was no master plan. I just wanted to write a column and all the rest followed. Still, I did have the support of some grand people along the way. My wife was always encouraging and still is. Bobby Branch gave me my first real break at the *Houston Home Journal* and provided me the stability of testing my skills. Millard Grimes became my mentor and gave me the push to expand into other papers and other areas.

Even today, I have people who are constantly helping me grow in my writing skills. Virginia Walton at the Houston and Peach bureau of the *Macon Telegraph* is forever being encouraging. Beth Milstead at the *Daily Sun* watches over all my writing there. And Debbie Hart took the big chance and put me on TV. Three great women and add to them my wife, who still is the reason I dare to take chances. With a strong love to rely on, all things are possible.

I was talking to someone the other day who was down in the dumps. He said his job and his life are blah. I tried to encourage him by showing him there were some positive things being overlooked. He finally agreed that his life was a 5 out of 10. Then he asked me how I would rate my life. I had to say (and I hope I am not tempting fate) that my life is a 10. I have my family, my faith, and my friends. Who could ask for more?

Here Comes the Flu

A new flu bug is going around, and believe me, it's the pits. I had it last week and thought I was going to die.

One of the worst things about it is how it sneaks up on you. I had worked all day, and then had my movie club. I got home a little tired but nothing out of the ordinary. I went to bed around 11:00 P.M. and slept like a baby. But about 1:30 A.M., I woke up suddenly.

My teeth were chattering so loud you would have thought someone was tap dancing in my head. And cold! Polar bears have better circulation than I was feeling at the time. I ran a tub of water so hot that I could have scalded myself easily, but, oh, how good it felt. I was cold down deep in my bones and that hot water seeped through my pores and warmed me from the inside out.

Finally warm again, I crept back to bed. Within minutes, I was burning up. Mount Vesuvius had erupted within my brain and lava was pouring through my veins. And so it went, freezing one minute and burning up the next.

All through the next day this hot/cold routine continued. All the while, I had no appetite, which for me is rarer than winning the lottery. I lived off orange juice and diet cola. Finally, two days later, I knew I had to eat something. My wife suggested Jell-O and I did eat some but I knew that wouldn't do. When she left the house to run some errands I waited a safe time and then snuck out to my favorite fast-food restaurant. I thought maybe a quarter-pounder and fries would be the best medicine.

This goes back to my take on the adage "Feed a fever, feed a cold, and feed anything else that is wrong with you."

During this bout with illness, I thought about how sickening it is being sick. It certainly isn't like being sick when I was a child. At the time (at least in my memory), I would rest in a bed with fresh linens, propped up on fluffy pillows, with a stack of comic books at my side. My mother would bring me various soups to help me feel better, and maybe a little ice cream to soothe an ache or pain.

In the afternoons, one of my friends would come over and we would play Monopoly or Clue to pass the time. And in between, there were the TV shows I liked. Ah, how nice it was to be sick—and miss school.

Nowadays, though, it's me and the cat, with no comic books and no games to play. Well, I tried her with Monopoly, but she kept wanting to sleep in the middle of the board. I might be missing work, but I'm worrying about what is being done in my absence. The weight of responsibilities is heavy on my mind.

One thought that does occur to me as I fight the fevers and chills is that life can turn around on you in a moment's time. One minute you are healthy and happy and the next you are in the pits. But even though I have been sick, even though I have had aches and chills and fever, even though I have missed work and had to watch countless hours of *Regis and Kathie Lee*, you know what? My life is still grrrrrreat!

Don't Sock It to Me

This may sound strange, but the older I get, the less I like socks. I guess it is a throwback to my high school and college days, but back then you either wore white athletic socks or no socks at all. Today I wear black or blue over-the-calf socks with my suits and no socks when I am informal.

Another thing that makes me anti-socks is the way they disappear from my sock drawer. A few months ago, in a fit of rage, I threw out all my socks and bought all new ones. Then as I put them in the dirty clothes hamper, I tied the two together. That, I thought, would solve my problems in trying to match up a shade of blue and black.

Yesterday, I went to get a pair of socks and all I had in the drawer were unmatched ones. Somehow, they had separated themselves from their mates and were single again. I hate when that happens!

Anyway, it is funny how fads and fashions hold on to us even when they have died out. In high school, it was necessary to wear "weejuns" (a form of loafers which may or may not still be around) and no socks. This made you the essence of coolness. In high school, of course, we had to wear socks to school so we wore the white ones, but in college, the bare foot was acceptable.

Even to this day, I feel most comfortable with loafers and no socks. But it drives other people crazy. "You don't have on any socks!" they exclaim like they are telling me something I don't know. I always want to reply, "Really? I didn't know."

When people observe my sockless feet, they usually follow up the "no socks" comment with one about the terrible cold I am going to catch. I don't put much credence in that prediction. I figure if I am going to catch a cold, it is going to come through my head where the hair is gone and I am hatless.

Lord knows, I try to wear hats and caps, but my family always begs me to take them off, as I look completely goofy. I don't know what it is about the shape of my head, but any hat or cap just sits there, looking undersized and askew. Now, the most ordinary of human beings can put a hat or cap on his head and look great. I alone am the "no cap wearer" of the Western world.

Another holdover in my apparel is the button-down collar. I just cannot wear a shirt that is not button-down. I have seen the styles change and have observed people wearing non-button-down collars who look fine. But for me, this is a fashion taboo. The few times I have received non-buttoned shirts as a gift and tried to wear them, I have felt as though the lapels were winging their way to glory.

Another fashion problem I have is with ties. I have become a real tie nut. I love them. I love the different colors and patterns. I like the way they look with sports shirts and formal shirts. I like ties! But ties don't like me.

If I tie my tie so that the bottom rests at the top of my beltline, then the back length of the tie is ridiculously short. And you can observe this shortness when the tie moves. Okay, I know you can tuck that portion into your shirt, but, to me, that looks goofy. I want to be able to have the two lengths of the tie be approximately the same, but it never happens.

I see people every day who have nicely tied, equidistant ties. They don't look like their bodies are shaped any differently than mine. But for whatever reason, I am tie-challenged. Mine just won't *do* right.

As I get older I seem to settle into a routine of clothing. I have tons of khaki pants, numerous blue button-down shirts and a couple of blue blazers. It is the Cooper uniform. It may get monotonous, but I never have to wonder in the morning what I am going to wear each day.

The years come and go, and certain things about my looks change. For one thing, I get bigger and balder. But as for clothes and dressing habits, the way I was is the way I am.

Things to Do in Denver

Last year there was movie called *Things to Do in Denver When You're Dead*. Well, I was in Denver a few weeks ago and luckily I wasn't dead, but I was bored. So herewith is my list of *Things to Do in Denver When You're Bored*.

Since I was without a car while at a conference at Hotel X, I ate at Hotel X, and I slept at Hotel X, I really didn't get a chance to see much of Denver, but I knew every inch of Hotel X.

For instance did you know if you stay in Hotel X and sleep in room 433 you can hear the elevators all night long? That little ding as the elevator stops at your floor can grind through your ears and into your brain prohibiting sleep of any kind.

And if you use your lunch break to go to your room and try to take a nap, did you know that housekeeping always cleans that room (your home away from home) between the hours of 11:30 and 12:30 each and every day. And if you ask if they can come back later, they give you the evil eye. It is downright chilling.

Then, if you decide to eat instead of sleep, the buffet offered is good but has strange combinations of food. I like shrimp and I like roast beef, but I don't like a combination of shrimp and roast beef. As I was fixing my plate, I scooped up what looked like an ordinary salad. Then I added some roast beef to my servings. When I started to eat, I found the salad

was a shrimp salad (they had been hidden), and that taste
clashed with the rich, juicy taste of the roast. It was enough to
set your teeth on edge.

While we are talking about eating, do you know just how
much junk food a body can absorb in a few days? This could
include grapes, cheese and peanut butter crackers, fudge
cookies, Oreos, and potato chips. And if you wash these down
with can after can of a diet drink, you won't feel guilty. Okay, a
little guilty—but not *that* guilty!

It is disconcerting, however, to have a mirror directly
across from your bed where you can watch your stomach grow
every day. You find yourself sucking it in when you catch a
glimpse of yourself, and then letting it out as you move to
another comfortable spot outside the range of the mirror. The
fat feeling returns with a vengeance because they give you
these teeny towels to use after your shower that won't even
stretch around your waist. You feel like you are made out of
Pillsbury dough…a lot of Pillsbury dough.

Finally, there was a drink machine located right outside
my door. On the one occasion I decided to order from room
service, I thought I might save myself a few cents by getting a
diet drink from the machine rather than paying the inflated
room service price. Imagine my surprise when I read the sign
on the drink machine:"Drinks—$1.00." Is that highway
robbery or what?

Regardless, I plunked my four quarters into the machine
and pressed the button for a diet drink. There was a hum, a
whirr, and then the orange drink light went on and out came
an orange drink. I was furious. Furious but dumb. Thinking
this was a one-time thing, I pushed the diet drink button
harder and then inserted another four quarters into the slot.

Same thing happened, and now I was the proud owner of two orange drinks.

I guess that is the way they do things in Denver, or at least at Hotel X.

Me and Billy Crystal

March for me means Academy Awards time. Yes, this is the month that I look forward to all year long. By this time, I have seen all the nominated movies and have picked my winners. But whether I am right or wrong is not the important thing. I just like seeing the Academy Awards show.

A few years ago, a friend of mine had a documentary film nominated for an award, so he got to go to the show. I was so envious and told him how much I had always wanted to attend. Well, he didn't offer me his ticket, but he did send me his program from the show and that was a very special gift. I read it from front to back and imagined what it must feel like to actually be there seeing all the stars.

At my house, this is the night when the answering machine picks up all the calls. I do not talk to people during the hours of the show. I just concentrate. My wife fixes me a special steak dinner and we sit in front of the set and comment on all the goings-on. Things have changed a bit. My wife is now a vegetarian, so she doesn't share the steak. Too, she usually goes to sleep before the show is over.

I have friends in Atlanta who have Academy Awards parties, but I have never attended one. The best one is a party where the guests dress up as a certain actor or actress in a role from the previous year. Can you imagine how that would tax the brain? Let's see, this year you could wear pretty ordinary clothes and be Jack Nicholson from *As Good As It Gets* or you could wear nothing at all and be a member of the cast of *The Full Monty*.

Some of my favorite Academy Awards memories include Louise Fletcher receiving the award for *One Flew Over the Cuckoo's Nest* and signing her acceptance speech for her parents, who are both deaf. Or Liz Taylor making her way down the aisle to get her award for *Butterfield 8* after nearly dying in London while making *Cleopatra*. I even got a kick out of Marlon Brandon sending a Native American to accept his award and to help protest his disagreement with the Academy Awards.

There have been great musical numbers (Burt Lancaster and Kirk Douglas singing a duet) and bad ones (Rob Lowe singing and dancing with Snow White). There have been good emcees (Billy Crystal, Bob Hope, and Johnny Carson), and so-so emcees (Whoopi Goldberg). But always there is that special something in the air that means you might have a streaker, or a political speech, or just a torrent of emotion.

A couple of years ago, I broke with tradition by not being at home for the Academy Awards. I was in Biloxi on vacation. I did manage to watch the show in my hotel room, and then quickly went back to the slot machines when it ended. It didn't seem the same not being at home for the special night though, so I vowed not to make any trips away from home during that time.

Still, this year I will be watching the awards away from Perry. I am going to host an Academy Awards party for the TV station where I work. Guests will come in costumes and there will be food and drink. We will all watch the show on a giant screen and I will make comments on the winners during the commercial breaks. It will be as close to a Hollywood event as I will probably get.

 Me hosting an Academy Awards party...my life just keeps getting better and better.

A Lifetime in High School

We only spend four years in high school, but somehow those four years set the pattern for our lives that follow. Four years, four short years, only the length of one presidential term, yet it seems like it lasts forever when we are going through these anxiety-driven times.

I actually entered high school in the eighth grade. At that time Clinton, South Carolina, had only a grammar school and a high school. I went from being a rule-the-roost seventh grader to the lowest-of-the-low eighth grader. We were called the sub-freshman and everyone else in the school was older and cooler than we were. We lived for the day when we would be ninth graders and could at least lord it over the eighth graders.

Then we got the word that when the next school year started there would be a new high school, one that encompassed grades nine through twelve. The eighth grade would be the top grade in junior high. That meant my class would go from being the lowest-of-the-low eighth graders to being the lowest-of-the-low ninth graders. It also meant that being in a new high school the upperclassmen would really think they were special and would work extra hard to make our lives miserable. And they did.

My high school class was average in most ways. We had some pretty smart people but none who broke school records. We also were a pretty divided class as to cliques and groups.

There was not a feeling of solidarity among us, but rather we stayed with our good friends and didn't venture out much to make new friends.

From the start, my two best friends had been, and continued to be, Hollis and Chuck. They were the ones I hung around with after school. My best friend, who was a girl, was Georgia. Georgia was the most genuinely friendly person I have ever met. She was so sweet and friendly that many people thought she was fake, but she wasn't. She had been raised to be a truly friendly person by her mother and she was that through and through.

Georgia and I had a radio show together. It came on every Monday afternoon and we told high school news and played a few songs. It was titled *Devils Den with Georgia and Jackie*. Our football team was named the Red Devils, and thus the name of the show.

That radio show was my big claim to fame in high school and it all came about because of Georgia. I think she thought up the concept, and I think she sold the radio station on the idea. I can't imagine me doing it on my own.

I do think you learn valuable life lessons in high school. You learn how to be ambitious, you learn how to make friends, you learn about love and life and how the two interrelate. It is a time of being your happiest and being your saddest, usually within a twenty-four-hour period. At least, that is how it was for me.

When my class graduated, it was one of the saddest days of my life. I was going to go off to college and I wouldn't have my security blanket of friends with me. I have never liked change, and I wanted my world to stay as it was, because by the time of my senior year I had finally begun to know my place in our microcosmic world.

High school was the best of times and the worst of times. It was four years of learning about ourselves, our relationships, our faith, our family, and our friends. After high school, we continued to learn but not with the intensity of those four years. What makes the years of our lives when we are fourteen through eighteen so important? Those are four short years, but we make memories that are never forgotten. Never.

What Is love?

Now that I have been married for twenty-eight years, I have decided I am an expert on love. Yes, and I am also the king of Siam. One thing I have learned is that love is not something you can define, predict, or even expect. It never happens when you expect it to happen, and it never acts in the way you want it to act. Love has a mind of its own.

When I was in high school, I fell for a cheerleader hard and fast. She was the prettiest girl in town and also the sweetest. She was also intelligent, moral, and fun to be around. My parents loved her, and I actually liked that they did. I knew others my age who didn't want their parent's approval.

When the cheerleader and I parted ways while I was in college, I went through my real searching for love phase. I dated older women, younger women, divorced women, women with children, and on and on. I just couldn't find anyone who suited me. And finally I just gave up. I don't mean I quit dating, I just quit looking for love, and of course that is when it found me.

I met my wife on a blind date. We dated for about a year and a half before we were married. She was still in college but we decided to go ahead and get married anyway. I was already out of college and law school and was serving in the Air Force.

We have now been married for twenty-eight years. That's amazing. I can't believe we have been married that long and still love each other the way we do. I think it might be even more than we did all those years ago. I know this: my heart still leaps when I see her walk into a room. Plus, she is still the person I would rather spend time with than anyone else.

What is the secret to our success? Well, in a word I would have to say it is communication. We talk to each other about everything. Both of us are analytical, and we like to hash things out. We talk about our likes, our dislikes, our hopes, our dreams, our greatest joys, and our greatest disappointments.

I honestly do think this is what holds our marriage together. Of course, it helps that we are in love. We are also best friends, and we share the same moral and religious views. All of those things are important, but somehow communication seems to be the main requisite.

I know couples who started out really loving each other but they never hashed out problems as they arose. They didn't want to hurt or upset each other, so they never had one of those "clear the air" conversations. Eventually, the stored up hurts and angers outweighed the love in their lives.

So if you are married, thinking about getting married, hoping to someday get married, remember the art of real conversation is the secret to success. Talk about everything whether it is comfortable for you or not. Get it all out there. It will pay off in the long run.

Love is a funny thing. You have to almost talk it to death in order to get it to live for a lifetime.

Old Is Whoever
Is Older Than You

When I was I in my teens I thought anybody over forty was old. In my twenties, I adjusted that definition to anyone over fifty. In my thirties, it was seventy and above, and in my forties, it was eighty. Now that I am in my fifties I don't think anybody is old unless they are a lot older than I am.

I think that is the way it will always be. Unless you're young, you don't think old age exists. You certainly never think you are old. That just couldn't be. Even if you have aches and pains, etc., that doesn't count. You may be in ill health, but you are never old.

When our children were little, we had a lady who babysat for us. Her name was Norine Jones. She was in her seventies when she started keeping the kids and lived to be in her eighties. A lot of people might have considered her to be old, but Norine didn't. She talked about old people, but they were always people who were older or looked older or even acted older than she did.

I remember one Christmas someone gave her a shawl as a present. Norine brought it over to our house and showed it to us. She was shocked and mortified that someone would give her such a thing.

"A shawl," she said. "Who on earth would think I wanted or needed a shawl? Shawls are for old women, not someone like me."

I think she was eighty-two that Christmas, so in calendar years some might think her old. Still in heart and in spirit Norine was one of the youngest people I ever knew.

People don't get old-looking any more. When I was a child, people in their fifties and above looked ancient. Old people were small, wrinkled, and gray haired. Today we eat healthier, take more vitamins, and have surgical procedures that can keep us looking young. Fifty is the new thirty, and seventy is the new fifty. You look at Hollywood and there are no old people acting in movies. The older actors and actresses have entered some kind of time warp or else they have a Dorian Gray type portrait up in the attic getting older and older every year.

The important thing is that we stay young at heart. That was Norine's secret. She was always interested in what was happening now. She didn't dwell in the past, although she had some great memories. She lived for today.

All of us get older with every day that passes but we don't have to be or act old. We can be young at heart and totally alive in the present. All those old people (those older than me) might not have this secret, but I do. So call me young!

What Might Have Been

Do you ever think of that one path in the road you might have taken that just might have changed your life? Or maybe that one opportunity you didn't get that could have made all the difference in the world? I think about these things sometimes because I hear so many people say, "if only..." I honestly don't have any "if onlys" I regret not having had, but I do sometimes think what turns my life would have taken "if only."

If only my mother had lived a longer life.... I don't dwell on this because I think God gave us almost a lifetime of closeness in the few short years we had. Still I wonder what my life would have been like if she had lived and seen me grown, married, and with children.

On the day I married I did have that yearning inside me for her to be seated in the front row and watching as Terry and I became husband and wife. I think she would have loved Terry, but I wonder what kind of mother-in-law she would have been. She was a force, and maybe she would have been one of those women who likes to retain a bit of control over her son's life after he's married.

I do know she would have been the best grandmother ever. She loved children and had a natural affinity for them. Even when I was small, she would talk about when I grew up got married and had "her grandkids." I do hate that my sons never knew her. They missed out on a wellspring of love.

If only I had decided on a writing career early on in my life.... Various teachers in my grammar school and high school career told me I had talent. Because of this, I did some writing for the school newspapers. But because no one told me I could pursue journalism as a career, I never even considered that option. Anyway, once I had said I might be a lawyer, the die was cast. There was such jubilation in my family over that possibility, I couldn't change careers at that point and disappoint them.

Still if I had started writing earlier I might have been more successful. Who knows what books and stories might have sprung from my mind. Perhaps I would have written the great Southern novel and been another Pat Conroy. Maybe.

I also think about what my life might have been like if I had married the cheerleader while I was in college. Aside from starving, would we have been happy? Would I have gone on to law school or would I have had to go into the military? And if I were in the military would I have been sent to Vietnam? Would I have survived and come marching home to my bride. Then, would we still be married all these years later, or would we not have been compatible? I can't imagine being married to anyone besides Terry, so it's hard for me to gauge my possible happiness with the cheerleader.

I am not a believer in predestination, but I do believe God has a plan for us all. Therefore I think all of the incidents in my life have been part of this master plan. It has worked out beautifully as each step I have chosen has led me to where I am today, and that is absolutely where I should be.

My mind might wander and ask "what might have been" from time to time, but I positively know what did happen was perfect for me. I am where I should be because of what did happen in my life, and I am a man with no regrets over what I might have missed.

Comfort Food for the Soul

When I think back to my childhood, I realize some of my warmest memories center around my church experiences. My family attended the First Baptist Church in Clinton, and we attended all the services. We went on Sunday morning and we went on Sunday night. I attended Royal Ambassadors and went to fellowship on Sunday nights after the church service. It made for a full day, but it was something I loved.

Everything in our life centered around the church. That was where most of my father and mother's social life was. There were always church suppers or receptions. People would jump at any excuse to bring food and sit down and eat. I think that is why I love those "everybody bring something" type of suppers to this day.

When I was old enough to date, we primarily dated to church. The cheerleader I dated all through high school and I went to the same church, so we always sat together on Sunday mornings. Then we would "date" to church on Sunday night.

When I was small, I would stretch out on the pew between my father and mother and go to sleep during the service. When I got older, my mother told me I had to sit up and listen to the sermon. If I didn't, she would nudge me constantly. My father, on the other hand, fell asleep during the sermon pretty regularly. But instead of nudging him and hissing "Wake up," mother would just pat his arm and let him sleep—unless he began to snore and then she would whisper, "Tom, you're snoring."

Daddy would wake and look around to see if anyone had noticed. Usually he would stay awake a few minutes and then go back to sleep. I couldn't figure out why it was all right for him, but not all right for me. That just didn't seem fair.

One day I asked my mother about it. She easily replied, "Your father is fine with the Lord. They are on good terms. So when your father goes to church he is totally comfortable with being there. He is such a good man that he doesn't have to worry that the Lord is upset with him. He can just relax and feel the comfort of the Lord around him."

"That's why he sleeps," she continued. "All of his worries from the week leave him and he is totally at peace. You, on the other hand, are still learning about the Lord and His ways, so you need to stay awake."

It made sense to me then and it makes sense to me now. Going to church is a comfortable thing if your life is in the right place. And the spiritual food you are fed through the sermon is comfort food for the soul.

So the next time you are in church and you see some people nodding off around you, think of this: they are so comfortable with their relationship with God that they are just absorbing some comfort food for their souls. They are absorbing it all even as they catch a short nap.

Epilogue

As I look back over these stories I am struck by how much happened in my life during the years 1996 thru 1998. The wedding of my son Sean was a major event and I am happy to report he and his wife Paula are now the parents of two children and live close enough to us that we get to see them often.

I am still covering the entertainment world for newspapers and television, so I still get the chance to meet a celebrity or two each year. This is one of those side dishes of life that are so delectable. I can pick and choose how much of this type of writing I do and that makes the avocation perfect.

Of course, since the years of this book I lost my father. He was kind and sweet until the day he died. I think my father's life always exceeded his expectations and that is the way it should be. All of us should be so fortunate.

For the past six years I have concentrated primarily on my writing. *Journey of a Gentle Southern Man* was published in 1999, *Chances and Choices* in 2001 and *Halfway Home* in 2005. These books have given me a chance to meet such fabled writers as Jaclyn Weldon White, W. Dale Cramer, Patti Callahan Henry, Mary Alice Monroe, Marjorie Wentworth, Charles Martin, Terry Kay, William Diehl, and on and on and on. I am in awe of the talent they each possess and bask in the glow of their respective careers.

My wife Terry and I have been married for thirty-six years now, which is amazing since she doesn't look a day over thirty-six. We continue to share a life that is fun, passionate, and totally enjoyable. All should be so lucky as to find their "soul mate" as I did.

Memory makers still happen in my life with regularity. And each time they do I place them in my journal for future reference. This book and all those before it came from that journal. It is what gave me the idea of collecting my stories in one place and having the collection published.

Yes, these are my memories, my stories, and ultimately my book. I hope you have found something inside these pages to warm your heart and fill your soul. I especially hope you have found a story that binds you to me and to all humanity. We are all in this world together and the ties that bind do not hinder us but rather make us united as we meet the challenges that come our way.

Until the next time our paths cross, remember I am a storyteller and I am the *bookbinder*.

Jackie K. Cooper
December 5, 2005